Great Promotion and Publicity Ideas for Youth Ministry

Zondervan/Youth Specialties Books

Professional Resources

Advanced Peer Counseling in Youth Groups
The Church and the American Teenager (Previously released as Growing Up in America)
Developing Spiritual Growth in Junior High Students
Developing Student Leaders
Feeding Your Forgotten Soul
Help! I'm a Volunteer Youth Worker!
High School Ministry
How to Recruit and Train Volunteer Youth Workers (Previously released as Unsung Heroes)
Junior High Ministry (Revised Edition)
The Ministry of Nurture
Organizing Your Youth Ministry
Peer Counseling in Youth Groups
The Youth Minister's Survival Guide
Youth Ministry Nuts and Bolts
The Youth Workers Promo Kit
110 Tips, Time-savers, and Tricks of the Trade

Discussion Starter Resources

Amazing Tension Getters
Get 'Em Talking
High School TalkSheets
Junior High TalkSheets
More High School TalkSheets
More Junior High TalkSheets
Option Plays
Parent Ministry TalkSheets
Tension Getters
Tension Getters Two

Special Needs and Issues

Divorce Recovery for Teenagers

Ideas Library

Ideas Combo 1-4, 5-8, 9-12, 13-16, 17-20, 21-24, 25-28, 29-32, 33-36, 37-40, 41-44, 45-48, 49-52
Ideas Index

Youth Ministry Programming

Adventure Games
Creative Bible Lessons on the Life of Christ
Creative Programming Ideas for Junior High Ministry
Creative Socials and Special Events
Good Clean Fun
Good Clean Fun, Volume 2
Great Fundraising Ideas for Youth Groups
Great Games for City Kids
Great Ideas for Small Youth Groups
Greatest Skits on Earth
Greatest Skits on Earth, Volume 2
Holiday Ideas for Youth Groups (Revised Edition)
Hot Illustrations for Youth Talks
Hot Talks
Junior High Game Nights
More Junior High Game Nights
On-Site: 40 On-Location Youth Programs
Play It! Great Games for Groups
Play It Again! More Great Games for Groups
Road Trip
Rock Talk
Super Sketches for Youth Ministry
Teaching the Bible Creatively
Teaching the Truth About Sex
Up Close and Personal: How to Build Community in Your Youth Group

4th-6th Grade Ministry

Attention Grabbers for 4th-6th Graders
4th-6th Grade TalkSheets
Great Games for 4th-6th Graders
How to Survive Middle School
Incredible Stories
More Attention Grabbers for 4th-6th Graders
More Great Games for 4th-6th Graders
More Quick and Easy Activities for 4th-6th Graders
Quick and Easy Activities for 4th-6th Graders
Teach 'Toons

Clip Art

ArtSource™ Volume 1–Fantastic Activities
ArtSource™ Volume 2–Borders, Symbols, Holidays, and Attention Getters
ArtSource™ Volume 3–Sports
ArtSource™ Volume 4–Phrases and Verses
ArtSource™ Volume 5–Amazing Oddities and Appalling Images
ArtSource™ Volume 6–Spiritual Topics
Youth Specialties Clip Art Book
Youth Specialties Clip Art Book, Volume 2

Video

Edge TV
God Views
Next Time I Fall In Love Video Curriculum
Promo Spots for Junior High Game Nights
Resource Seminar Video Series
Understanding Your Teenager Video Curriculum
Witness

Student Books

Going the Distance
Good Advice
Grow for It Journal
Grow for It Journal Through the Scriptures
How to Live with Your Parents without Losing Your Mind
I Don't Remember Dropping the Skunk, But I Do Remember Trying to Breathe
Next Time I Fall In Love
Next Time I Fall In Love Journal
101 Things to Do During a Dull Sermon

Great Promotion and Publicity Ideas for Youth Ministry

Over 140 easy-to-use ideas that really work

Les Christie

Zondervan Publishing House
A Division of HarperCollins*Publishers*

Great Promotion and Publicity Ideas for Youth Ministry
Copyright © 1994 by Youth Specialties, Inc.

Youth Specialties Books, 1224 Greenfield Drive, El Cajon, California 92021, are published by Zondervan Publishing House, 5300 Patterson S.E., Grand Rapids, Michigan 49530

Library of Congress Cataloging in Publication Data

Christie, Les John.
        Great promotion and publicity ideas for youth ministry: over 140 easy-to-use promotion and publicity ideas that really work / by Les Christie.
            p.   cm.
        Includes index.
        ISBN 0-310-49091-X (pbk.)
        1. Church work with youth. 2. Church publicity. I. Title.
    BV4447.C478 1994
    259' .23--dc20   94-8113
                                                                        CIP

Edited by Noel Becchetti and Lorraine Triggs
Design and typography by Rogers Design & Associates
Cover illustration by Corbin Hillam

Printed in the United States of America

94 95 96 97 98 99 /CHG/ 10 9 8 7 6 5 4 3 2 1

TABLE OF CONTENTS

DEDICATION

To Eastside Christian Church, where I had the privilege for 22 years to serve as youth minister. I am taking with me a backpack full of cherished memories of people and places. Leaving you is the saddest part of this step.

AND

To San Jose Christian College, where a new adventure has begun as chairman of the Youth Ministry Department. I want to thank you for making the transition such a smooth and pleasant experience. I'm looking forward with great anticipation to our journey together.

ACKNOWLEDGMENTS

Some of the publicity and promotion ideas found in this book originally appeared in the *IDEAS* Library, published by Youth Specialties. Others were collected, stolen, pilfered, borrowed, adapted, copied, appropriated, and plagiarized by the author from youth workers around the country, and from magazines, tape recordings, conversations, conventions, and the walls of the men's room at the Texaco gas station in Fullerton, California. Some ideas were even written by the author.

The author wishes to thank the following creative youth workers who originally developed these ideas and contributed them for publication. Without these people, this book would not have been possible. Thanks again to: Ed Bender, Michael Berry, John Blackman, Jill Bourne, Darrel Brock, Brian Buniak, Joe Burlingham, Grant Byrd, Lida Clancy, Richard A. Cooper, Bobbi Cordy, Dan Craig, Robert Crosby, Len Cuthbert, Tom Daniel, Carol Eklund, John Elliott, Denny Finnegan, Jay Firebaugh, Dave Gallagher, Robert Garris, Paul Gearhart, David Gilbert, Cindy Warner Gorman, Joseph A. Greer, Lyle Griner, Roger Haas, Connie Hamilton, Ken Harrower, Milton Horn, Marion Hostetler, Bob Hunt, Tim Jack, Rick Jenkins, Darrel Johnson, Jack Jones, Sylvan Knobloch, Jim Larson, Mike Leamnson, Paul Lewis, Kathryn Lindskoog, David Lynn, David Mahoney, Doug Mathers, Russ Merritt, Clay Nelson, Bill O'Connor, Ken Owen, David Parke, Calvin Pearson, Ray Peterson, Scott Phillips, Russ Porter, Joey Potter, Eden Prairie, Dan Pryor, Patsy Quested, Jim Ramsey, Steve Redmond, Larry Rice, Frank Riley, Carolyn Roddy, Paul Sailhamer, Ben Sharpton, Mark Shoup, Bobby Shows, Mark A. Simone, Mark Smith, Christopher Snow, Karen Spray, Ed Stewart, Andy Stimer, Bill Swedberg, Greg Thomas, Mark Thompson, Dana VanCleave, Todd Wagner, Marjorie Walsleben, Jim Walton, David Washburn, Don Warner, Kimberly Weast, Bryant Wilson, Ray Wilson, Len Woods, Marty Young, and Mike Young.

Every youth worker struggles with how to get the word out about his or her youth ministry to the kids in the community. This book is designed to provide practical, helpful insights into how to get the job done, whether your church has a large budget, a small budget, or no budget at all. This book contains dozens of ideas that have been tried and tested throughout the country. This is not a theory book, but a how-to book. This book will help you reach more teens for the Lord as you attract more kids to the variety of programs you offer during the year. It has been said that you can lead a horse to water, but it doesn't have to drink. Yet, you can feed the horse salt and motivate it to drink. This book is designed to be the salt to encourage kids to attend and participate in youth activities.

This book will also help you to build a positive image of your youth group in your church, area schools, and the community. When people think of your church's youth ministry, it will be in an affirmative, positive manner.

The typical reason a youth group advertises is to gain new members, persuading people to attend who have never attended before. However, in many youth groups, I have found that publicity and promotion tends to be informative, rather than persuasive. The groups rely on word of mouth to achieve persuasion, and use publicity and promotion primarily to build awareness. In this book you'll find dozens of ideas on how to both inform *and* persuade. You'll find tons of ways to communicate what you have to offer to the kids in your community. Your youth ministry may be the best-kept secret in your area; this book will help you get the message out.

Although this book is about effective youth ministry promotion and publicity, I don't want you to focus on "marketing" at the expense of developing servant leadership, striving for spiritual maturity, and seeking godliness in our lives and in the lives of our students. The Bible states clearly, "Unless the Lord builds the house, its builders labor in vain" (Psalm 127:1a). This verse tells me that the Lord needs to be in the center of everything we do, including promotion and publicity, and all we do needs to bring glory to the Lord.

In the end, the most attractive publicity is the consecrated, dedicated, loving lives your teens demonstrate on their campuses. Your most effective and efficient marketing tool is the changed lives of your kids. We need to call teens to deeper spirituality, encouraging them to develop spiritual disciplines and pray for spiritual renewal. Your youth group not only needs a new publicity idea; it also needs spiritual sensitivity. We need teens who have pure hearts and a sincere faith.

The best publicity is a group of turned-on young people who support their group. Fire up those kids! Make them feel worthwhile. Enthusiasm is contagious—nothing can replace excited people.

I'm glad that you picked up this book. It means that you're serious about building a more effective youth ministry. It's one of the greatest callings any Christian can aspire to, and I'm looking forward to sharing what I know about promotion and publicity to help you reach more young men and women for Christ. Are you ready? Let's go!

Les Christie

SECTION ONE:
THE BIG PICTURE

How to Use This Book

This book was written with the church and parachurch youth worker in mind; however, the promotion and publicity ideas found here will also work with other youth organizations—school groups, scout troops, clubs, sports teams, and after-school programs. The success of your promotion and publicity depends to a large extent on the effort you place in prayerfully choosing, planning, and following through on your promotion. Many promotions fail because groups do not carefully analyze their past and current experiences. You need to seek the right idea at the right time for your group.

Rushing to grab an idea or two because they look quick and easy can actually hurt your promotion of an activity. Carefully select the ideas you will use. Youth groups must have a plan and direction, along with a reason for selecting a particular idea.

Skim through the ideas in this book, and treat yourself to an "idea smorgasbord." Select ideas that are best suited for your group. An effective publicity idea is one that works for your particular group. Out of the over 140 ideas in this book, I hope that you will be able to use at least twenty to thirty of them.

As you survey the ideas, brainstorm how you could modify some of them to fit your group's needs. Be as creative as you wish at adapting and strengthening the ideas you find in this book. Think of ways you can strengthen existing promotional and publicity ideas.

CHOOSING THE RIGHT IDEA

How can you select the right promotion and publicity ideas for your group? There are no hard and fast rules, but here are some questions to help guide your decision-making process:
• What are the needs of my group?
• What has and has not worked in the past?
• How will this particular idea help to meet those needs?
• Do we have the resources to make this particular idea work?
• Can we afford to do this idea financially?
• Will this idea work with my size group?
• Will this idea violate any ethical rules of my group?
• Does this idea fit the personality of my group?
• How will my group respond emotionally to this idea?

I selected the promotion and publicity ideas for this book that I felt almost any group could use; however, some of the methods may be sensitive or controversial for your group. Some may even be offensive. The best way to avoid problems is to use good judgment. If you have reason to believe a particular idea is going to cause problems, think twice before you use it. Sometimes the damage done by going ahead with a questionable idea outweighs the potential good.

Finally, *always* inform parents and your supervisors of your promotion and publicity ideas before you use them. Let them know what you hope to accomplish, and how you intend to get there. This step will keep you out of some deep weeds and save you potential grief—not to mention your job.

Staying Legal and Ethical

chapter 2

You may be stealing someone's property without realizing it. Many youth groups shamelessly copy articles, photos, and artwork without permission. Appropriating copyrighted material without permission is against the law. It is stealing. It is a federal offense punishable by fines and, in some cases, imprisonment.

Copyright owners make their living by receiving compensation from each person who uses their material. Making unauthorized copies is like sneaking into a ballpark or a movie without paying. This is a bad example for the young people we are trying to reach with the Gospel.

Just because you buy one copy of an item doesn't give you the right to distribute it to others. It would be similar to buying one airplane ticket and expecting the entire youth group to be able to fly on that one ticket.

Some have excused their behavior by saying they were doing God's work. A woman, at a convention where I was speaking, once grabbed about $75 worth of my books. As she was walking off with them, she whispered in my ear, "The Lord told me that I could take these books for my youth group." I stopped her and whispered back, "But the Lord didn't tell me." Jesus told His disciples in Luke 10:7, "The worker deserves his wages." If everyone made illegal copies of copyrighted material, publishers and authors could not stay in business.

If you want to copy material from a book, magazine, or other media, write to the publisher or producer of the material for permission. Most are happy to grant you permission for free or a nominal fee. The amount varies from company to company and author to author, depending on the agreement the publisher has with the author.

You may also be able to purchase, at a nominal cost, the right to use the material on an overhead. Most companies are glad to work with you, but you need to ask. If you get permission, make sure you observe its limits. Don't abuse the privilege!

GUIDELINES FOR SEEKING PERMISSION

• Be honest and specific about how you intend to use the items, including how you or your organization will benefit—financially or otherwise.
• If the answer is no, graciously abide by that decision and look for alternatives. For example, find an artist in your church who'll create a logo for your group.
• When you've received permission to use something, ask what permission line the company requires and display it word for word on whatever you produce.

If you've pirated copyrighted information, wipe the slate clean and ask the publisher's or producer's forgiveness. You'll be surprised at the positive response you get. Be prepared to accept the consequences of standard fines or a harsher penalty, particularly if you've profited by using the stolen work.

Prior to your "copycat" confession, talk with your ministry's administrator and an attorney. Also, stop using any pirated material in your possession!

A Primer on Effective Promotion and Publicity

chapter 3

A s you prepare publicity for your youth program, keep three goals in mind. First, you need to get the young people to read and react to your promotional efforts. The postcard that kids trash without reading accomplishes nothing. The computer-generated banner on the youth room wall that no one notices does no good either. The information must reach your kids' conscious minds so they can decide about their involvement in the program or event.

Second, you want your publicity to generate interest. Some kids look at a flyer, see the topic, and immediately want to participate. These young people probably are already active in the youth program or have a vested interest in the event. But many other teenagers who receive your publicity piece haven't decided whether or not they want to attend. For these "on-the-fence" young people, your publicity needs to create a desire to participate in the upcoming program. While you can accomplish this in many ways, the message, "If I don't go, I'll miss something really special" needs to come through.

Third, you want your promotion and publicity to generate results. A major mistake many youth groups make is to spend money on advertising without establishing a way to ascertain whether or not the expenditure was worthwhile. Before you budget funds for promotion and publicity, have some reasonable means for determining what type of return you hope to receive from your investment. Set a specific, measurable goal you hope to accomplish. For example: "We want our publicity for the Back-to-School Hamburger Bash to bring ten new kids to the event." A specific, measurable goal can help you determine what publicity efforts will help you reach that goal most effectively.

WHERE DO I START?

You can come up with a quality piece of publicity if you think through the entire project before you produce anything. For example, you want to design a flyer to tell your youth group about an upcoming meeting on sex and dating. Now that you have your topic, list everything that comes to mind that relates both to your topic and to the youth culture. Brainstorm how current movies, songs, TV shows, commercials, magazines, and real-life situations can be used to publicize your event. Nothing at this point in the creative process is too dumb or too crazy to rule out.

After coming up with several ideas for different themes and formats, choose the one that most creatively and effectively communicates your message. Determine the best attention-getting headline. Be sure your piece gives all the necessary information (who, what, when, where, why, and how), and what the reader should do next (come, contact, call). Before actually writing your announcement copy, study ads in popular youth magazines.

KEEP IT SHORT, SWEET, AND SIMPLE

The first sentence you use in a letter, handout, or poster should jump out, grab the readers, and stimulate their imaginations. If the opening does not intrigue them, they will read no further.

Minimize your word content. In some cases, musical groups and personalities need no introduction—their names alone will carry the piece. For others who need a brief introduction, give an honest, positive, and imaginative statement. Don't water down your message with a lot of extraneous words, logos, or excessive use of photos. Keep your message strong, clear, and simple.

HOOK THE READER WITH GRAPHICS

While graphics—artwork, cartoons, fancy borders, cute letters—are one of the last things you consider in the creative process, it's the first thing your reader will see. An appealing promotional piece could have a border or other graphics that highlight the message area. Important information such as dates, times, and place could be underlined, boxed off, or printed in big, bold type so it stands out from other parts of the copy.

Any artwork, no matter how amateurish it may be, is better than no artwork. Don't let the lack of good artwork keep you from designing effective promotional pieces. If you stop and think about it, there are several sources for art: illustrations from books, cartoons from magazines, old encyclopedias, magazine ads, old textbooks, posters, catalogs, junk mail, coloring books, the phone book yellow pages, children's storybooks, calendars (for numbers), comic books, simple illustrations from newspapers, cartoon-type greeting cards, and even paper placemats from restaurants. (Remember: *always* seek permission before using copyrighted material!)

COMPARE PRINTING OPTIONS

Compare different printers, since estimates for printing jobs may vary widely from one printer to the next. Don't forget to check with the larger printers in your area—sometimes they can do the job for less than a quick-print shop. Also, check out the print shop in your high school or local vocational center. The instructor may be able to do a quality print job for you at a much lower cost than most print shops, but you may have to wait longer for the finished product.

Photocopying is the great standby if you need something printed quickly. However, large numbers of copies can get pretty expensive, and artwork and photos don't reproduce that well on a photocopy.

One last item to take into consideration: if you plan to mail a piece without using an envelope, keep in mind that the post office won't accept anything smaller than 3 1/2" x 5".

APPEAL TO YOUR KIDS

Here are some tips to help you keep your promotional pieces lively and attractive to your audience:

• *Make advertising appeal to youth.* This should be kept in mind in every detail. Consider their interests, their desire to have things a little different from the everyday, and their fast pace of living.

• *Be different!* If there is anything that appeals to youth, it is something out of the ordinary. Place your copy sideways, upside down, slanting or crooked; anything to make it eye-catching, yet readable. When it's different, youth will love it and read it too! Inexpensive rubber stamps can quickly add a theme, logo, or comment to the outside of an envelope. Phrases such as "Alert", "Caution: Exotic Animals Inside", or other zany slogans can add excitement to your publicity.

• *Make it catchy.* What catches teenagers' eyes? The chance to win a new cassette or CD? Ways to be popular and successful with the opposite sex? You can splash ideas like these across the outside of your envelopes to build curiosity in your kids. Remember, it costs no more to print all over the envelope than it does to print only the return address in the corner.

• *Make it humorous.* If it's funny, kids will read it. Even if the event itself addresses a serious topic, humorous publicity often creates the additional enthusiasm needed to convince kids that the event will be worth their time.

• *Make it attractive.* Remember that your publicity pieces compete with thousands of others that kids see each month. Your promotion needs to look sharp.

• *Make it easy to read.* Your printed materials may get only a quick glance, so display the information according to its importance. Use big type for the really important information. The rest of the details can be in regular size print on the back or inside of a brochure or flyer.

• *Make it visual.* In addition to making your publicity attractive, you need to create a strong visual effect. Catchy pictures, artwork, and color all contribute to a good visual piece. Often I've included photos of kids at previous similar events. If you do use photos, pick ones that convey excitement and interest.

• *Make it hard to throw away.* If your youth calendar is attractive enough to hang up, the chances that kids will read it increase dramatically.

• *Make it diverse.* If possible, your youth newsletter should never look quite the same twice. This will help kids avoid the habit of glossing over the material and dropping it in the trash. If something about it looks different, it gives the impression of offering something new inside.

BE CREATIVE WITH YOUR MATERIALS

Think creatively about paper, for example. Instead of an endless stream of 8 1/2" x 11" sheets of paper, try some of these ideas:

• If you're traveling somewhere and plan on taking brown-bag lunches, print information about the trip on the bags and send them to everyone.

• Print a message about an upcoming Mexican dinner on tortillas and then mail the tortillas in envelopes.

• Planning a hiking trip, bike trip, or athletic event? Have a rubber stamp made that includes the basic information (date, time, place). Most office supply stores can make inexpensive rubber stamps, with three- or four-line messages. Stamp the message on an old white sock and mail the sock.

• Whenever I travel by air, I collect vomit bags from the airplanes. When a kid in the group has a birthday, I write a personal greeting on the vomit bag and send it to him or her. Kids love them.

TAKE ADVANTAGE OF NEW TECHNOLOGY

My typewriter is now a relic that won't fetch five bucks at a garage sale. The church's current copier shrinks or enlarges my flyers by one percent increments, edits out unwanted clutter, sorts, collates, staples, runs ten million copies, and microwaves my dinner. Meanwhile, I spend hours each week staring at the screen of my entry-level personal computer—all in the name of youth ministry.

Yessiree, things have changed. Although I have very little idea how this rectangular box on my desk works, I've found that it actually is a productive tool for youth ministry. This thing really does boost my efficiency and effectiveness as a youth worker. I've found all sorts of practical ways for my computer to enhance my promotion and free up more time to spend with real kids. Here are a few ways the computer has helped me:

• I used to hand draw most of my flyers, or would find an artistic someone in the church to do them for me. I had a file full of rub-on letters that would inevitably rub off on each other. Occasionally, when I wanted an especially sharp-looking brochure or poster, I would "send it to the printer." It came back looking great, but I had no idea how it got that way. (I discovered later that they used a computer.) Now, with word processing, drawing and painting programs, and desktop publishing, I can do a reasonable job of making this stuff all by myself—complete with fancy fonts, borders, boxes, and shading. And it takes less time than the handwritten ones took.

• Remember traditional clip art? All youth workers worth their salt have at least a volume or two of youth-ministry clip art. You simply find the drawing of the water skier slamming into the dock, paste it onto the front of your summer camp flyer, and you're guaranteed a successful camp promotion. Clip art is now available on computer software and CD-ROM (a compact-disk storage device). For example, Youth Specialties has all six volumes of the *ArtSource*™ clip art series available in both IBM and Macintosh formats. Just scan through the selections, select the appropriate art, and transfer it to your brochure. By using drawing or painting programs, you can edit or alter the existing artwork.

• Although "database management" may sound terribly corporate and clinical, in reality it's just organizing and sorting—precisely and quickly. You can compile a detailed database of your students—including mailing labels, phone lists, attendance and follow-up tracking, students' interests and activities, and more. I used to hate messing with addresses and phone lists. I always forgot somebody, or mailed one student three letters and another student none. Now, if I want a list of all the seniors from El Dorado High or all the junior high girls or all the birthdays in chronological order, it just takes a few keystrokes and I have what I need. Divide your young people into natural groupings and appeal to each on the basis of needs and desires.

   You can organize your database into groups of:
• Youth who already attend
• Youth in the church who don't attend
• Youth who came to church, but stopped attending

- Youth related to church members
- Friends of youth in the church
- Youth who live in the neighborhood
- All youth who have attended your denomination's statewide convention

KEEP A PROMOTION IDEAS FILE

Never discard an idea that could be used in promotion. Store it somewhere so you can come back to it later. You'll be surprised how often you'll return to those creative bursts of genius.

INVOLVE YOUR STUDENTS

Delegation is critical because it is almost impossible for your students to develop maturity, competence, or leadership apart from involving them and giving them responsibility. This includes promotion and publicity. It's their youth group and they must have a sense of ownership. Delegation is challenging. If the ball is not handed off properly, it can easily be dropped; the program suffers, demoralized students feel like failures, and already burned-out youth workers become even busier as they mutter, "If you want something done, do it yourself."

Successful delegation is not a one-step process. Many youth workers have found these four steps helpful in implementing a process of delegation:

1. *I do it* (preparation). I have knowledge about promotion and publicity. I can communicate that knowledge to others.

2. *I do it and you watch* (partnership). The training process has begun. The potential leader is gaining knowledge by observation.

3. *You do it and I watch* (coaching). The shift has occurred. The responsibility has shifted into the hands of the trainee and I am now in the position of an encouraging observer. I exercise patience to avoid rescuing potential

failures and provide encouragement and feedback.

4. *You do it* (delegation). The process has now reached the delegation point. The odds of success are much higher because of the training.

Don't do anything for young people that they are capable of doing themselves. Otherwise, you will make them emotional cripples always relying upon you, never learning to trust God, and never discovering the opportunity for valuable personal growth. Just ask Becky.

We had an important activity coming up that we hoped would attract a lot of non-Christian kids, and Becky was responsible for publicity in our youth group. Becky, however, only completed half of the publicity and left it, unfinished, with a note on my desk. She was hoping I would finish it for her.

I called her home and left a message with her mother, explaining that the publicity was Becky's responsibility and that if she didn't do it, it wouldn't get done. Becky didn't complete it, and only half the number of kids we were expecting showed up.

The following Monday, Becky came into my office. I asked her what happened. She explained that she felt she had let the whole group down. I agreed and asked what she thought she should do next.

"Maybe I should quit," she responded.

"Quit?" I replied.

"Well, maybe I shouldn't quit," said Becky.

We talked about responsibility and commitment. Becky saw how she could change her priorities and schedule in order to get things done. We prayed together that God would use her. Becky was a dynamite publicity chairperson from that day on. I could always count on her. (Postscript: Becky is now a missionary with her husband and children in Chile.)

STAY FOCUSED

Much more can and will be said about generating effective publicity throughout the book. If you keep the basic principles of this chapter in mind as you develop your promotional ideas, it will help you stay focused on the goal of your publicity efforts: getting your kids to know about your activities, and getting them interested in participating in them.

Happy publicizing!

SECTION TWO:
HOW TO PROMOTE AND PUBLICIZE IN YOUR CIRCLES OF INFLUENCE

Promoting in Your Church

chapter 4

I f your youth ministry is invisible to the rest of the congregation, it's time to turn some heads. You must get the word out to the entire church. If you don't, you may be astonished one day when you are questioned by church leaders about what the youth group is doing, or how money for youth ministry is being spent.

The promotional ideas in this chapter will help your group to get the congregation's attention, and you will have a great time being noticed. The church will better appreciate the youth program, and many adults may want to get involved in supporting your youth activities.

ALL-CHURCH YOUTH MEETING

Invite the congregation to participate in a regular youth group meeting. Have group members lead mini-discussions and activities as if they were speaking to their peers. Play your favorite youth group games. Advertise the event as a chance for church members to transform themselves into teenagers for a night!

B.O.M.B. SQUADS

B.O.M.B. stands for "Bring Our Members Back!" and it makes a good theme for a drive to contact inactive members of your youth group. Small groups of kids form "B.O.M.B. squads" and visit, write letters, or make phone calls to kids who, for one reason or another, have stopped coming to the youth group. You might want to throw a "B.O.M.B. Blowout" party and invite old members back to the group, or create "B.O.M.B." T-shirts for your group to wear at school.

Another possibility is to involve other groups in your church in this campaign. You could fly a large helium balloon above your church with the word "B.O.M.B." written on it. (Of course, it would be a good idea to run this idea by your evangelism committee first!)

BUTTON BOOSTERS

Buttons group members can wear to church, school, or work are inexpensive and invaluable marketing tools. A little creativity and a button-making machine is all you need for your group members to wear advertising wherever they go.

You can order a machine through Badge-a-Minit, 345 N. Lewis Ave., Box 800, Oglesby, IL 61348, or call 1-800-223-4103.

CELEBRITY ATTENTION

Enlist the support of big-time movie and rock music personalities. How? You can obtain life-size posters that theaters and movie rental and music stores use to advertise new movies and records. If you explain your purpose to the managers of these businesses, they will usually give these to your group once their own advertising campaigns are completed.

You can then take these life-size posters and create your own promotional campaign by having the stars endorse your upcoming event. For example, make a cutout cardboard speech balloon and have Amy Grant say, "Can we count on you to support our . . . ?" You get the picture.

CHURCH HISTORY

Have kids visit longtime church members and interview them about the history of the church. Next, have kids compile these stories into a scrapbook of your church's history. Each year, update the book. Once a month, during a regular church service, read a short story out of the history scrapbook.

CHURCH NEWSLETTER

If your church has a weekly or monthly newsletter that is mailed out to the entire congregation, have a regular column in it about youth group activities. Have the teens write it. Mention names. Kids and their parents like to read about themselves and others in the group.

COMMITTEE MEETINGS

Invite several of your church's or organization's "string-pullers" to your youth committee meetings. Also, reserve general church committee time to tell about kids who have grown through your program. Encourage kids to tell about their spiritual growth at other church gatherings.

FRONT PEWS

Arrange with the ushers to have your group members sit in the front pews for each church service. This is a good way to gain visibility.

MUG-SHOT WALL

Kick off the year by plastering a church wall with profiles and photos of all your group members and volunteers. Find a black-and-white striped shirt, and have each person wear it for his or her picture. Paste the photos on wanted posters that list kids' hobbies, interests, ages, grades, and other pertinent information. Add kids' "parole dates" (when they graduate from high school). Decorate the wall with bright colors and Christmas lights to draw attention to it.

PARENT PROGRESSIVE DINNER

For an evening, arrange to borrow the kitchens of church members who aren't parents of teenagers. Form teams of teenagers to plan, purchase, and prepare a special progressive meal for their parents. Use each host home as the site for a different course of the meal. This is a good way for church members to mix with your kids, your kids to mix with other adults in the church, and your parents to feel appreciated by one and all.

SPONSOR SWEEPSTAKES

In the day of $10,000,000 sweepstakes, methods of recruiting sponsors for retreats, camps, and lock-ins may need an update. For example:

YOU HAVE BEEN CHOSEN AS A POTENTIAL WINNER IN THE FIRST BAPTIST YOUTH MINISTRY

DISCIPLE NOW WEEKEND HOST HOME CONTEST

To determine if you'd like to be a winner, simply call (toll free) Tim Davis at the church office (368-4793).

Prizes for the lucky GRAND PRIZE WINNERS include:
• Two luxurious nights with young people from our church!
• Cash for any meal purchases!
• Excellent cuisine prepared and provided by youth parents and youth workers!

CALL TODAY!!!
NO PURCHASE NECESSARY
VOID IN ALL STATES EXCEPT MISSISSIPPI

We need your help! If you are interested in serving as a Host Home for our Disciple Now Weekend March 1–3, or if you have any questions about Disciple Now, give Tim a call.

WORSHIP PARTICIPATION

Have your group members participate each week in the regular church services as readers, singers, speakers, or ushers.

YEARBOOK SLIDE SHOW

Throughout the year, have kids take slide pictures of youth group events. As an end-of-the-year celebration, put together a slide show with original music and skits. Present the show to the congregation.

YOUTH ARREST

Here's a way to familiarize the adults and the noninvolved youth in your church with the youth group. Have several of your young people or adult leaders dress up like police officers. Arrange with a local law enforcement agency or a costume rental company to get enough uniforms so two "officers" can be at each entrance to the church. You might want to hook up a traffic light in front of the church entrance or, if you can make additional arrangements with the police department, park a police motorcycle by the door.

As every teenager enters the church, tell him or her that he or she is under arrest for being a high school student. Take these kids aside and give each of them a summons to appear before Youth Court, which is in session the night of your youth meeting. When families without young people enter, briefly explain what you are doing and tell them about your youth group.

The summons could say something like the following:

Certificate of Summons

You, _____, are hereby and forthwith placed under arrest for being in the _____ grade. Your arrest is made possible because of the long arm of the law handed down in the decision of the Supreme Judge in His very historic case in John, chapter 3, verse 16. You are hereby and forthwith summoned to appear in court before the Judge <u>(Youth Minister)</u> on September 21, in the basement of the Nativity School Courthouse. Youth Court will start at 7:00 p.m. sharp, where you shall be given a three-minute trial. (Since the judge is known as "Hang 'em High_____," your trial will be very short!) You will be sentenced to eat pizza and laugh a lot . . . but not before working on the Judge's chain gang for about an hour in a trade-up scavenger hunt. If you wish to plead your case, you are free to bring a teenage lawyer friend who did not appear at church today.

Signed,

_____
Senior Officer

_____

_____
Junior Officers

YOUTH MONTH

Plan a month of events that involve the congregation in the youth program. Use some of the ideas in this book and add your own (such as group-sponsored potlucks, talent shows, nature hikes, and so on). Make your all-church youth month an annual event.

YOUTH REPORT

During your church's regular announcement time, set aside time for your kids to present creative announcements of upcoming events (using pantomime, skits, dances, and so on). Chapter Ten has plenty of good announcement ideas.

YOUTH SERVING OTHERS

Plan a monthly service project for group members to help church members with yard work, house painting, or other activities. Advertise the service in the church newsletter, and have teenagers make periodic announcements during your regular services.

Promoting in Your Schools

chapter 5

Your students need to know they are free to openly express their religious beliefs in the school environment. While school administrators may impose reasonable restrictions on when, where, and how, students also are allowed to distribute religious literature on their campuses. Many other modes of evangelism are available to students. If your schools grant permission for other outside clubs to use bulletin boards, the school newspaper, or even the P.A. system for announcements, then your kids may have the right to use these means too.

Youth workers are finding access to the public school campus increasingly difficult to obtain, despite the fact that the Supreme Court has upheld the rights of students and teachers to express their religious views, and the passage of the Equal Access Act. In light of this trend, we must learn to be flexible. We must think of new and creative strategies for gaining access to the public school campus and maximizing our student contacts.

Here are some promotional ideas that will work with most schools' access policies:

ASK SOMEONE WHO KNOWS

This is a one-and-only, all-purpose poster idea. No matter what you want to advertise, this poster will do it. Why? Because it contains no specific information whatsoever, but simply states: "Ask Someone Who Knows."

If you wish to advertise on a school campus, for example, hang copies of the poster all over school, and have the kids from your youth group wear little stickers which read, "I know."

The principle is fairly simple: Kids see signs around the school that tell them to ask someone "who knows." Next, they notice your kids wearing "I know" stickers, so they'll ask what it is that your kids know. Of course, your kids will then unload all the information about your next meeting or special event. Instruct your kids to give an "I know" sticker to each person who comes up to them, because now he or she knows too! It is an intriguing and effective means of advertising. This idea works well when a school does not allow religious or church posters on campus. The poster really says nothing to offend anybody.

BOOSTER PLACARDS

Here's a good way to build a positive image for your youth group on campus and build school spirit at the same time. Print up booster placards, 11" x 14" or so, with a "Go Team!" slogan on one side, and general information such as the team roster or team schedule on the other side. Also include an announcement for your youth group, and a final statement of support for the team and the school.

Print the placards on heavy cardstock and use the school's colors. Get permission from school officials ahead of time; then have your kids pass the placards out to all the fans at a football game.

If you like, print something humorous on the back of the placard, such as:
• Raise this card and holler to show your support!
• Form a card section with others who also have these cards.
• Use this card as a collar-shaper for your shirts!
• Use this card to line your cat's litter box.
• Use this card as an umbrella if it rains.

CONTEMPORARY CARD HANDOUTS

One of the most effective ways to advertise a youth program or event is to print up a handout for kids to pass out to their friends at school. It is more personal than posters and less expensive than the mail.

One type of handout that is always a winner is one that not only informs, but also entertains. The handouts described here get the message across, and also contain a joke or humorous story to lead the reader into the advertisement. The handouts are patterned after contemporary greeting cards, but don't have to be nearly as large. The front of the card carries the grabber line, and when the card is opened, the punch line to the joke is inside. The back of the card can be used for your announcement.

The best way to produce these is to have someone draw the artwork for the joke and the advertisement, and then take it to a print shop that does quick printing. A good size for this type of handout is 8 1/2" x 5 1/2" (half of a letter-sized sheet), folded once, so it measures 5 1/2" x 4 1/4".

Following are several joke ideas. I've included the grabber line, the punch line, and a short tie-in line that can be used with whatever you are advertising. Use as much creativity as possible when designing your handouts, and don't limit yourself to these jokes. If you hear a good joke, it just might work on a contemporary card handout.

Grabber line: I taught my pet fish to sing for you, but lately he's been singing off-key.
Punch line: And you know how hard it is to tuna fish.
Tie-In: There's nothing fishy about . . .

Grabber line: Latest clinical tests proves that seven out of ten doctors . . .
Punch line: leaves three.
Tie-In: Already proven . . .

Grabber line: Choose your favorite nose: (pictures of noses)
Punch line: Now if you're through pickin' your nose . . .
Tie-In: Blow on over to . . .

Grabber line: Just so I wouldn't forget to tell you this, I tied my shoelace around my tongue.
Punch line: Now I've got athlete's mouth.
Tie-In: Don't forget this . . .

Grabber line: They say that success is ninety percent perspiration.
Punch line: If that's so, you must be a tremendous success.
Tie-In: A program that's one hundred percent successful . . .

Grabber line: The other day I saw a man who looked like he hadn't had a bite for weeks . . .
Punch line: so I bit him.
Tie-In: Put the bite on your friends to . . .

Grabber line: I bought you two authentic pearl buttons from the South Sea Island of Bali.
Punch line: Now you'll be the only guy in town with two pearl Bali buttons.
Tie-In: "Isle" meet you at . . .

Grabber line: Beautify junkyards . . .
Punch line: throw away something lovely today.
Tie-In: A beautiful program . . .

Grabber line: Stop! If you have any brains at all, you won't open this card!
Punch line: Well, that settles it.
Tie-In: Brains or no brains, come to . . .

Grabber line: Get ready, get set,
Punch line: get lost.
Tie-In: Get on down to . . .

Grabber line: "Johnny, can you drive with one hand?"
          "Sure, baby!"
Punch line: "Then wipe your nose, it's running."
Tie-In: Drive on down to . . .

Grabber line: Before you hang your clothes,
Punch line: make sure they get a fair trial.
Tie-In: Hung up? Meet the gang at . . .

Grabber line: Always cross the street with the light.
Punch line: That is, if you can rip it out of the pavement.
Tie-In: Rip on down to . . .

Grabber line: Here's a couple of real dillies:
Punch line: Dilly, dilly.
Tie-In: A real dilly of a program . . .

Grabber line: How to get ahead
Punch line: (Picture of a guy chopping some guy's head off with an ax)
Tie-In: You'll laugh your head off at . . .

Grabber line: Note the sad story of the flea
Punch line: They all go to the dogs.
Tie-In: You can go to . . .

Grabber line: This morning I got up, shaved, showered, and splashed a little toilet water on my cheeks . . .
Punch line: and then the lid fell and hit me on the back of the neck.
Tie-In: Fall in at . . .

Grabber line: "My girl is one of twins."
            "Really? How do you tell them apart?"
Punch line: "Her brother wears glasses."
Tie-In: An unmistakable program . . .

Grabber line: How do you get down off of an elephant?

Punch line: You don't, stupid, you get down off of a duck!
Tie-In: Head on down to . . .

Grabber line: Open in case of fire.
Punch line: Not now, stupid, in case of fire!
Tie-In: A program that's really hot . . .

Grabber line: "Hey, how come you're pulling that chain?"
Punch line: "Man, did you ever try pushing one of these things?"
Tie-In: Push your friends to be at . . .

FIFTY REASONS TO BELONG TO A CAMPUS BIBLE CLUB

Add a cartoon to this list, and then use it as a handout, a mailer, or bulletin board display.

1. To study the Bible.
2. To be with friends.
3. Rutabagas will absolutely never be served for refreshments.
4. It's nonfattening.
5. It could prevent flat feet.
6. To have fun.
7. You don't have to wear water wings to participate.
8. It's better than doing homework.
9. It isn't at 5:00 a.m.
10. To grow in your faith.
11. There are no finals.
12. You may win valuable prizes.

13. Brussels sprouts will never be served as refreshments.
14. To meet new friends.
15. To play silly games.
16. We need you.
17. The leaders care about you.
18. It is almost never fatal.
19. There are no homework assignments.
20. For support.
21. Ten out of ten doctors recommend it.
22. To help plan things that you want to do.
23. It has the Good Housekeeping Seal of Approval.
24. Like Mt. Everest, it's there.
25. It is a known cure for the mid-week blahs.
26. (For girls) Guys are there.
27. (For guys) Girls are there.
28. It doesn't cause bad breath.
29. To be with other Christians.
30. It's free.
31. For fellowship.
32. It contains absolutely no cholesterol.
33. Ren and Stimpy think it's great.
34. There are people who want to listen to you.
35. Your youth leaders will do all your homework for you. (Just kidding.)
36. *Beverly Hills 90210* and *Marvin* aren't on then.
37. To share ideas.
38. No previous experience is required.
39. You will get mail.
40. You will have lots of dates. (We'll send you a calendar.)
41. You will like it.

42. To learn more about God.

43. We give double coupons.

44. You are important.

45. There has never been a major earthquake in the meeting room.

46. While it contains no fluoride, it has never caused a cavity.

47. To come and pray together.

48. To get to know each other.

49. It is not lite.

50. After you have taken time to read all fifty of these reasons, you may as well give it a try. See you at Bible Club at noon on Wednesday in room ____!

FOOTBALL CARDS

This idea is good for outreach, building relationships with local schools, and group identification. Every fall, print up each local high school's football schedule. Use each school's colors, and print its schedule on wallet-sized cards. On the back, put information about your youth group, a phone number kids can call, and perhaps a simple explanation of salvation. Make these cards available to the schools to distribute, and for your kids to pass out to friends.

HERE'S MY BUSINESS CARD

Traditional business cards work well among professionals. Create one that your kids can distribute to their friends on campus.

Leave room for a kid's name and phone number as well as a list of your group's activities.

INVITATION TO THE PRINCIPALS OFFICE

If you live in a town where one of the school administrators attends your church, have that school official call each kid in your group out of class to come to their office. The kids will be scared to death, wondering what they have done. When they get to the office, he or she encourages them to attend a certain activity at your church. Your kids will be blown away.

LOCKER POSTERS

A favorite pastime of many junior high and high school students is decorating the inside of their lockers. Kids plaster them with pictures, pins, stickers, license plates, concert posters, and tickets.

You can use this to your advantage by designing creative posters, tailored especially for the inside of a locker door. Get the measurements from your local campus (the average high school locker door is 12" wide) and design a poster that your kids will be proud to display. It can promote the youth group or just be a positive poster that encourages kids to share their faith with friends.

WITNESS ADS

Here's a great way to advertise your youth group and give your kids an opportunity to share their faith in a concrete and meaningful way.

In one of the local high school newspapers, place an ad for your church's youth group, and feature the testimony of one of your youth who attends that school. Ask key kids to write short statements on why they believe in

Jesus, along with a verse of Scripture. Make sure these kids feel OK about being published. This approach will not only promote your group and share the Gospel, but will encourage your kids to walk their talk.

YOUTH GROUP BOOK COVERS

To promote your youth group at school, print up some attractive book covers for your kids' textbooks. Come up with a good design for the front that your kids like, and print your youth group name and logo on the back. Give several covers to the kids in the church to give away free of charge to other kids at school.

Promoting in Your Community

chapter
6

L et your community know what your youth group is doing. Successful youth ministry spreads the word outside the church grounds. You can gain respect for your youth program with solid promotion in your community.

BE A GUEST

If you have a newsworthy story, get invited to be a guest on a local radio or TV talk show. You may find the free publicity you receive a boost to your ministry. Since these shows often schedule guests weeks and even months in advance, contact the station managers early.

BUS BENCH BACKS

Many cities rent bus bench backs for advertising. You can rent this space for a remarkably reasonable rate in many cities.

BUSINESS BILLS

An effective way to spread the word about your event is to create hand-bills that can be placed in the lobbies or other high-traffic areas of local businesses. You can target a large number of potential visitors by placing flyers at your local supermarket, doctor's office, or bookstore.

CHEAP CLASSIFIED

Most communities have a *Penny Saver*-type classified newspaper in which your group can place inexpensive (or sometimes free) ads.

COUNT THE WAYS

A good publicity campaign that gets results includes several different types of promotion. People in the community need multiple exposure to your upcoming event in today's world of media bombardment. You need to tell people what you are doing, remind them that you are doing it, jog their memories a time or two, and then tell them again so they won't forget. A good rule of thumb is the seven times rule: Tell people seven different ways to guarantee adequate promotion.

CREATE A NEWS EVENT

Sometimes you can attract the attention of the local media by creating a news event geared especially for them. For example, one group of young people wanted to dramatize how polluted a nearby river was. The kids scooped out a few gallons of the dirty water and carried it to the state capitol. There they poured the water into small plastic bags, and handed the ugly packages to startled passersby. The local TV stations had a heyday filming the reactions of the recipients of the filthy water. And the young people made their point.

Many youth groups have received superb publicity in the newspapers about their mission trips or service projects. For instance, a community newspaper might love to run pictures of your group from a mission trip to Mexico. Events like Walks for World Hunger bring Christian service to the attention of the community.

FLOWERS TO SECRETARIES

Send flowers to secretaries in schools and businesses you frequent on Secretaries Day. If you can't get past the secretary, you usually can't get to the kids or to the boss.

FREEBIE POSTER BOARD

Your group can save money on publicity by asking local merchants (music stores, video rental stores, department stores, fast food restaurants, grocery stores) if they'll save the posters in their windows for you. You can use the reverse side of these posters to create your own posters. You'll have done your recycling duty and saved yourself money on materials as well.

GROCERY BAG PROMOTION

This idea combines public service with advertising aimed at the general public. See if a local supermarket will allow your youth group to work for a day bagging groceries for customers and carrying the groceries out to their cars for free. Make sure kids who do the bagging get instructions on how to place the groceries in the bags so they won't crush anything.

In each bag of groceries, with the permission of the supermarket, drop a flyer advertising a church event (car wash, spaghetti dinner, canned-food drive). It's a good image-builder and a great way to advertise.

NEWS RELEASES IN LOCAL NEWSPAPERS

Your goal is to produce publicity material that can be used by the paper without excessive editing. The less rewriting an editor has to do, the better.

• When preparing a news release, always remember to include the "who, what, where, when, why, and how" at the beginning. Never wait until the end of your release to spring a surprise or give important information. Typically, news is written in the style of an "inverted triangle"; the most important information appears at the beginning of the release and the least important details are found at the end. If an editor needs to eliminate copy because of space, he or she can start cutting from the *bottom* of the release, leaving the most important information intact.

• Use short paragraphs. Two or three sentences are usually plenty.

• Do not editorialize. Do not write, "The M.Y.F. will be serving delicious ice cream and mouth-watering pizza." Words such as "delicious" and "mouth-watering" are value judgments and have no place in most news releases.

• Always type your news releases. Double-space your material, and type only on one side of the paper.

• Begin typing half-way down on your first sheet. Number your pages.

• Always put a contact person (usually you!) and phone number on your releases in case the editor has a question or needs more information. Type this in the upper right-hand corner.

• For most events, the best time to submit your release is one week beforehand. Call your local paper to find out deadlines for community events.

• Readers usually pay much more attention to photographs than to printed words. Whenever you can, submit photos with your stories. Use black and white prints—not slides, color snapshots, or negatives.

• Always include picture caption information with photos. It's best to attach a slip of paper to the back of the photo that has the typed information about

who or what appears in the picture.
• Good publicity includes people's names. People relate to people, not events. Most people like to see their names in print. It acknowledges their presence and communicates appreciation for their support.
• Sometimes you may get better responses from newspapers if you deliver your releases and photos in person. That personal touch may be enough to make the editors want to help you.

PHOTOS WITH SEASONAL THEMES

Editors of community newspapers are always on the lookout for pictures with seasonal themes. If your group is going to have a Valentine's party, the black-and-white picture you take while the gang decorates might work well as a theme picture in your local paper. Seasonal pictures are valuable only before the holiday; there isn't great demand for a patriotic photo on July 5.

PUBLIC SERVICE ANNOUNCEMENTS

Public Service Announcements (PSAs) are another means of gaining media exposure for your event. Your group can write a PSA about your cause or event that lasts ten to sixty seconds. Contact your local TV and radio stations and submit your announcements to their regular rosters of community events.

SECTION THREE:
GREAT IDEAS FOR PROMOTION AND PUBLICITY

Mailers

Young people receive less mail than adults, so they usually get excited when something arrives in the mail for them. This might lead some people to believe that kids read everything they get. Unfortunately, that's not always true. With exposure to multi-million dollar advertising campaigns on television and in magazines, many young people are forced to filter what they read and how they respond to advertising.

Your regulars will read your advertising in whatever form it comes. But youth workers with a missions mindset need to create materials that catch the eyes of kids who have little or no commitment to Christ or your youth ministry.

ABSENCE EXCUSE

The following absence excuse may be used as an alternative to the old "We missed you last Sunday" postcards. Mail it out with a return envelope and wait for the response.

Please fill out and return in the enclosed envelope immediately.

Dear Youth Director,

I was absent last Sunday because: (check one)
___ I was adding up my telephone bill and fainted.
___ My folks added up my telephone bill and fainted.
___ My dad strained himself ripping out my phone.
___ My clothes were in the washing machine.
___ I was in the washing machine.
___ My folks were on restriction and I was watching them.
___ I took out the garbage and the trash collectors took me by mistake.
___ My tricycle is in the garage for an overhaul.
___ I went flying over the weekend and my arms were tired.
___ I was mugged by an old lady.
___ I don't have a good excuse like those above, so I will be there this week to make up for my absence.

Sign your name: _____

Seriously, we miss you when you are not with us. Hope to see you at church this week.

Here's a great idea for a promotional letter to mail to all absentees:

Dear _____,

We sure hope xhax you can be wixh us xhis nexx Sunday ax xhe Firsx Bapxisx Church. Because xhis is xhe vacaxion season, many young people have been gone. We wanx xo keep going xhis summer wixh a boom in axxendance. Come Sunday and lex's go over xhe xop for Jesus. By xhe way, I guess xhax by now you are wondering why we have lefx oux all of xhe Ts in xhis lexxer. Xhe reason is xhax we've had so many absenx Ts laxely, we jusx didn'x have enough xo use in xhis lexxer.

DON'T BE AN ABSENTEE SUNDAY.

ACTION HANDOUT

Next time you want to advertise your youth meeting in a unique way, try this. Design a handout that folds in half. On the front, put anything you want, as long as it is attractive and invites kids to open the handout and look inside. Inside the handout, print an assortment of puzzles, games, tongue twisters, and the like. On the back of the handout, print all the details of your upcoming event. This handout is good because it not only gets your message across, but also gives the kids a bit of a challenge as well. For added fun, supply the answers to the puzzles at the meeting, and award prizes to those who got them all correct.

ADVELOPES

Every week or so, you glance at the pile of old magazines in the corner of your office. You never use them, but you're loathe to toss them because—well, you never know when they might come in handy.

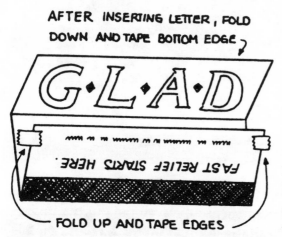

AFTER INSERTING LETTER, FOLD DOWN AND TAPE BOTTOM EDGE

G·L·A·D

FAST RELIEF STARTS HERE.

FOLD UP AND TAPE EDGES

Here's an immediate way to use the colorful page ads—especially the ones in Christian music magazines. Carefully tear out the ads, and fold them into envelopes in which to mail announcements for special activities. Simply fold the ad in thirds and use the top third as the flap. Tape the sides first and the flap last. Use a white self-adhesive address label so that the address will not be lost in the design. Each member of your group will get an eye-grabbing, customized, one-of-a-kind envelope.

AIR MAIL

Want to remind kids of commitments they made at the last retreat? Or remind them of a big upcoming event? Look no further for an enthralling way to send short, quick notes to your kids. For each note, inflate a light-colored balloon and tie it off with a paper clip or rubber band (so you can deflate it easily). With a fine-point, permanent-ink marker (to prevent smudging), write your note on the balloon. You may want to use phrases like "pumped up," "air mail," or "lots of hot air." Deflate the balloon and mail it in an envelope.

When your kids receive their balloon notes, they'll either need a magnifying glass to read them—or figure out that they need to blow up the balloon to get the message. Chances are, kids won't forget the message.

BAG INVITATION

Next time you want to invite your group to a sack lunch meeting, here's a great way to do it. Use an ordinary lunch bag as an envelope. Put the invitation inside the bag and staple it shut. Put the address on the bag and mail it. The invitation can read: "Bring your lunch in this bag to . . ." and fill in the time and place of your meeting.

BIBLE STUDY BLURB

Here's a fun way to generate excitement for a Bible study group.

Mailers

Something similar to this example could be printed on any size sheet of paper and mailed or passed out to the kids.

HOW BIBLE STUDY CAN CHANGE YOUR LIFE...

BEFORE I STARTED GOING TO BIBLE STUDY I WAS POOR, ALONE, AND THOUGHT THAT JERICHO WAS A NEW ROCK GROUP. I USED TO SIT HOME TUESDAY NIGHTS WATCHING T.V. AND THINKING I WAS HAVING FUN OR PRETENDING I WAS DOING HOMEWORK.

FINALLY I HIT BOTTOM. A FRIEND TOLD ME ABOUT BIBLE STUDY. AT FIRST IT WAS HARD SEEING ALL THOSE PEOPLE HAVING FUN, LEARNING NEW AND INTERESTING THINGS, AND MAKING SO MANY NEW FRIENDS AT ONCE. BUT I GOT USED TO THAT.

I STARTED TO FEEL THE BENEFICIAL EFFECTS THE FIRST WEEK. NOW I KNOW THAT JOB IS AN OLD TESTAMENT BOOK AND NOT JUST SOMETHING YOU DO TO MAKE MONEY.

NOW I'M HOOKED ON THE BIBLE STUDY HABIT!

WON'T YOU JOIN ME? EVERY TUESDAY NITE AT 7:00 P.M.

BLOW-UP ANNOUNCEMENT

Next time you need a clever handout idea, try this one. Print up a card that folds in half (like a greeting card). On the front of the card print this message: "Don't open this card!!! It will BLOW UP!!!"

Inside the card, tape a balloon, and print your announcement.

BULK MAIL

Make your mailings cost-effective. If you have 300 or more people who should receive youth group mail, you can save money by sending your mail bulk-rate. Check with the post office about bulk-mailing procedures and costs for nonprofit organizations. Have more than 150 pieces of mail, but less than the required minimum for bulk mailing? Send each person on your list two pieces or more. It still may end up costing you less.

CALLING CARDS

Think up humorous or just plain weird business or organizational names to precede your return address or the mailing address. The smiles you'll

---

Mailers

generate just might increase your readership. For example:

> Anointed Worm Ministries, Inc.

> If God can use a worm, He can use you.
> Jonah 4:7

> Elvis Is Alive International Headquarters (use this for your Elvis lovers)

> Mozart Is Alive International Headquarters (use this for your classical music lovers)

Or, instead of being comical, you could add an affirming touch to the outgoing address:

> Maker of Marvelous Melodies
> Jill Reynolds

Or use affirming title such as:

> Wonderful Grandparents
> Pat "The Patient" Jones
> Harry "Helpful" Brown
> Gene "Gentle" Smith

When addressing mail to kids, avoid anything even remotely derogatory, negative, or uncomplimentary about a person's physical appearance, behavior, habits, family, or cultural background (e.g., Mark "Meathead"

White). Nor should you flatter; be sure the statements are sincere and accurate. Choose only those phrases you can back up with reasons—because the kids themselves will inevitably ask for evidence of the virtues you assign them.

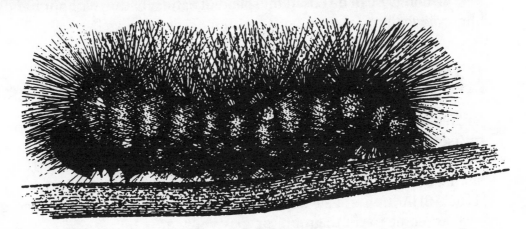

CATERPILLAR EATING CONTEST
We Provide The Caterpillars

This idea is a real attention-grabber. Make some posters and send out a mailing, advertising a "Caterpillar-Eating Contest" at your next youth event. Be sure to include the note, "We'll provide the caterpillars!" The kids will be anticipating a relatively gross activity.

When it comes time for the contest, bring out the "caterpillars", which are actually ice cream-free banana splits. These can be made individually or in a long trough.

Here's the recipe (you'll need enough bananas for each of your kids):

Split a banana lengthwise and place it flat-side down on a plate. Spray long stripes of canned whipped cream down the back and sides of the banana. Decorate it with green sprinkles and chocolate syrup stripes. Use pretzel sticks to make feelers, two cherry halves for eyes, and rows of raisins for feet.

The contest can be based on speed of eating, eating without hands, blindfold feeding, or team consumption. Kids will love it.

COMMANDMENT CARDS

Here's an idea for a get-well card or an announcement you can print up yourself and customize for each young person. It can be printed on regular 8 1/2" x 11" paper, folded in thirds the long way. On the front flap, draw a picture of Moses or the stone tablets and print the words, "It is written, 'THOU SHALT' . . . ." Leave space underneath to complete the message, such as "come to youth group" or "pay your camp bill."

When the card is opened, the inside flap could read, "Where is it written, you ask?" Then, that flap opens and the inside reads, "Page one of this card!" Below that, leave space for specific details or a personal message.

ENGRAVED INVITATION

Have you ever heard someone say, "He would need an engraved invitation before he would come." Well, go ahead and send the person an engraved invitation. You don't have to use costly paper, just be sure you use the words, "Engraved Invitation," and make it look fancy. For a special touch, use the folders photographers use for mailing enlargements as the invitation envelopes. You can buy these quite inexpensively. Whoever receives one of these engraved invitations will get the message right away.

GET OUT THE GLASSES

Send a flyer in the mail—but instead of filling it with information, leave the flyer blank except for a 2" x 2" section in the corner that contains all your information in tiny print. You can make it tiny on your original by reducing it a few times. The kids have to get out a magnifying glass to read what it says.

LETTER FROM AFAR

Teenagers are usually impressed when they receive a letter from a foreign country. Make the most of it by having someone you know in another country mail your kids letters, announcing a coming event. Provide the person who will mail the letters with the information you want communicated, addresses, and money to cover postage.

This is an especially appropriate idea for a meeting with a missions emphasis. Have missionaries write letters to your kids, encouraging them to attend the meeting or, better yet, to visit their countries. If kids receive a letter postmarked from somewhere such as Zimbabwe or Honduras, it will really get their attention.

As long as you are taking the time to prepare a letter, it may as well be a good one. It costs no more (usually) to be creative. The ideas presented here have been used successfully. Adapt these samples to fit your own needs, with your own information, names, dates, or whatever.

Youth Group I. Q. Test

Match the items in the column on the left with the ones on the right:

1. **Last meeting**	a. **location for next youth group meeting**
2. **Lippo residence**	b. **before Christmas holidays**
3. **Sweaty armpits**	c. **a man laughing his head off**
4. **Monday, December 16**	d. **our youth director**
5. **Goes "ha, ha, ha—clunk!"**	e. **our next big party**

Score: 5 right—genius, 4 right—above average, 3 right—average, 2 right—slightly out of it, 1 right—beyond help, 0 right—comatose

Regardless of your condition, there's a place for you at our next get-together THIS MONDAY NIGHT at Lonnie Lippo's house, 4801 Vista Sombrero Drive, beginning promptly at 6:33 p.m. BE THERE!

Dear Student,

A routine check of school records has disclosed that you failed to complete kindergarten. We must, therefore, call to your attention Municipal Regulation 55-2938.11:

> KINDERGARTEN MUST BE COMPLETED BY EVERY RESIDENT OF THIS COMMUNITY. THIS MANDATORY REQUIREMENT FOR A RESIDENTIAL PERMIT CANNOT BE WAIVED UNDER ANY CIRCUMSTANCES.

Your lack of kindergarten certification causes us to hereby order you to report for kindergarten registration on the first WEDNESDAY before the new term begins. In view of your advanced age, however, it will not be necessary for you to bring along your mommy or daddy. Registration for the coming semester starts this Wednesday night.

To Whom It May Concern:

The Traffic Ticket Accounting Bureau wishes to inform you that its records indicate an overpayment on your part for traffic tickets. We cannot refund this overpayment, but you could do us a favor by quickly running up some other traffic violations so that we may balance our books. Therefore, we strongly urge you to speed on over to the next exciting meeting of . . .

What goes, "Ho, ho, ho—clunk!"?
Answer: Santa Claus laughing his head off.

"Yule" laugh your head off at the next exciting meeting of TEEN CLUB, next Wednesday night at 6:30. Don't miss it!

The All-Purpose Letter

Check one box for each category:

Dear:

☐ *Granny*
☐ *Fingers*
☐ *Alvin*
☐ *Fungus breath*

Just wanted to tell you that I have been:

☐ *watching my weight.*
☐ *in love with my history teacher for the past two years.*
☐ *picking my nose and thinking of you.*
☐ *washing my socks.*

After reading this letter, I hope you:

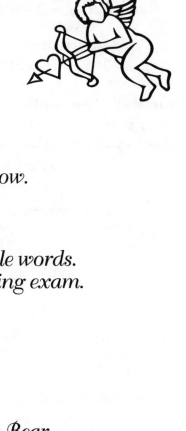

☐ still feel like calling me "Poopsie."
☐ get paroled soon.
☐ brush your teeth.
☐ fall out the nearest three-story window.

Well, I have to close now because:

☐ I don't know any more three-syllable words.
☐ I need to study for my basket-weaving exam.
☐ my mother is going to dress me.
☐ my nose is bleeding.

Signed:

☐ Mel Gibson
☐ Mama Bear, Papa Bear, and Baby Bear
☐ Your mother
☐ Energizer Bunny

P. S. Youth Fellowship next Sunday night, 6:30 at the church.

CONGRATULATIONS!!!

You are one of the lucky winners in our exciting
"WIN A BUCK" contest!

Your male deer will be sent to you under separate cover. If, however, you do not receive your buck by next Tuesday, bring this card to the special winner's meeting at Kathy Hoaky's house, Tuesday night, 7:00 p.m. sharp.

Now that I have your attention . . . I'd like to remind you that next week HI-LIFE will present a provocative program entitled, "Is Sex a No-No?"

If you fit into one or more of the following categories, you need to come.

(Check all those that apply to you.)

____ You went to the drive-in movie last weekend and can't remember what movie you saw.

____ You wish you had a club on your last date.

____ Your boyfriend keeps taking you to see the "submarine races" at the river.

____ Your girlfriend likes to date in groups . . . of fifty or more.

____ You believe in making out on the first date.

____ You believe in making out before the first date.

____ Holding hands turns you on.

Even if you don't fit into any of the above categories, you'll fit right in at HI-LIFE. The meeting starts at 7:23 p.m. sharp! See you there!

Campus Club Social Intelligence Test

Here is your personal copy of the Campus Club Social Intelligence Test. It will determine just how much fun you are at a party, and will show you the areas in which you need to improve.

Circle true or false:

True False   Kissing is when you grab another person's right hand with your right hand and shake it vigorously.

True False   The best way to be the life of the party is to stand against the wall, with one foot against it, looking cool.

True False   The most acceptable way of getting another glass of punch is to dip your own cup into the punch bowl and joke, "Well, we all have the same germs, anyway."

True False   The proper time to leave the party is at three o'clock in the morning, or when the hostess' father comes down the stairs with a shotgun, whichever comes first.

To check your answers, bring this test to the next meeting of Campus Club, which just happens to be this Thursday night at 7:00 p.m. We may wind up having a party of our own! Don't miss it!

THIS POSTCARD ENTITLES YOU TO ONE FREE NIGHT IN THE COUNTY JAIL (TAX AND TIP EXTRA).

IN ORDER TO RECEIVE THIS VALUABLE FREE OFFER, FOLLOW THESE STEPS:

1. WRITE DOWN THE IMPORTANT ADDRESS BELOW AND KEEP IT.
2. CRUMPLE THIS CARD INTO A LITTLE BALL.
3. CRAM IT DOWN THE THROAT OF THE NEAREST POLICE OFFICER.

═══════════════

This postcard is also good for one great evening at Youth Fellowship in case you decide not to take advantage of the free offer. Meet us at Bob Frit's house, 4040 Yucko Street, at exactly 7:13 p.m. See ya there.

═══════════════

You May Have Already Won a Valuable Prize!!!

Here is your lucky number: 3 4 5 6 7 8

If your lucky number matches the winning number below, which was drawn at random (of course), then you may have won all or none of these exciting prizes:

1. An all-expense, one-way trip for two to Temecula

2. An autographed picture of our local mortician
3. Three tickets to the Museum of Antique Lawn Mowers
4. One pound of minced raccoon livers

Here is the winning number: **3 4 5 6 7 8**

If your lucky number matches the winning number you may, or may not, have won the lovely prizes. For further instructions, bring this card to our next Hi-Life meeting this Wednesday night, 7:00 at the church.

MESSAGE IN A CAPSULE

First, buy empty capsules at a drugstore. Because of drug restrictions, you will need special permission from the pharmacist. Second, type the same three-line, single-spaced message until you have enough messages for each member of your group. A sample message could begin: "Feeling bad lately? Need medicine to pick you up? Here's good news about a picker-upper. At MYF Sunday, the program will be. . . ."

Third, cut the messages into strips, tightly roll them, and put one message into each capsule. Finally, place the capsules into pre-addressed and pre-stamped envelopes for mailing. You can imagine how it feels to open a large envelope and find a tiny capsule. Once kids figure out that they have to open the capsules, they'll get your message.

MIRROR MASK

Another great attention-getter is to send a flyer that only can be read by looking at it in a mirror. On one side, it can say:

> This is your message, should you choose to read it! There is a message on the back of this letter. The only way to decode this message is by looking through the two eyeball holes on the front and peering into a mirror. The people of the Old Testament—the Hivites, the Moabites and the Mesquitobites used this method of decoding in ancient times—so it's biblical! (See Hezekiah 4:7, 8.)

On the opposite side is your announcement, printed backwards. Cut holes for the "eyeballs," so kids can hold up the paper and look through it. And don't forget to add a special illustration for that personal touch.

MISSING PERSONS REPORT

The following letter idea can be used to follow up on absentees. Print it up and check the appropriate boxes when it is mailed out. You'll have to add some information, such as the person's name, the date, etc.

Missing Persons Report

Missing person's name:

☐ Murgatroyd Fluglehorn   ☐ Eddie Vedder
☐ Michael Jordan   ☐ Attila the Hun
☐ Batman   ☐ (type person's name here)

Last seen in the vicinity of:

- [ ] the Huntington Beach Pier
- [ ] the middle of the freeway
- [ ] Fred's Bar
- [ ] Snoopy's doghouse
- [ ] the Red Star Fertilizer Plant
- [ ] (type name of your church here)

On:

- [ ] a tricycle
- [ ] a date with Winona Ryder
- [ ] time
- [ ] (type date last attended here)

Last seen wearing:

- [ ] nothing
- [ ] a smile
- [ ] Tarzan's loincloth
- [ ] red and blue tennis shoes (one of each)
- [ ] a wet suit

Reported missing by:

- [ ] David Letterman
- [ ] the Easter Bunny
- [ ] Troy Aikman
- [ ] your mother
- [ ] the I. R. S.
- [ ] (type name of your group here)

Signed:

- [ ] Ronald McDonald
- [ ] Barney
- [ ] (type your name here)
- [ ] Mickey Mouse
- [ ] Uncle Sam

NEWSPAPER WANT ADS

Send a postcard to your kids that instructs them to look in the "want ad" section of your local newspaper on a certain day to find out what the youth group is doing that week. The ad can be inexpensive, and it's a great way for kids to find out about an upcoming activity.

PIZZA PARADE

With a dictionary or thesaurus—and some alliterative knack—you can create some fun announcements for events. Here's a sample letter that was sent to members of a youth group:

Dear Group Member,

You and your peers are invited to a Pizza Parade.

"What in the pink pizzazz is a Pizza Parade?" you ask.

A Pizza Parade is
- plenty of pizzas of all proportions properly prepared by prominent persons of perfectly pompous prestige
- properly praised pizza in a picturesque and palatable presentation
- popular and poetic project promoting a proper perspective and the Prince of Peace

"Sounds pretty peppy, not to mention powerful," you pronounce perfectly and precisely.

Pre-register for this party by October 10 with the paltry pile of two dollars.

"Preposterous!" you say.

Perhaps. But for you to partake in this particular pizza production, we press you to persuade your parents, pull in your peers, and present your person in either purple or pink.

Proudly practicing persuasion,

(Your name)

Here are samples of some creative alternatives to the typical "we-missed-you" postcards sent out by Sunday schools around the country. Print these cards on colored card stock and use them for absentees or for attracting new kids. The postcards will give your group a more personal touch. Better yet, have some of your talented kids design some postcards for you and the group.

POTATO PRINTING

Here is the cheapest and easiest method of printing your group can do. Here's what you need:
• some large potatoes, cut in half
• small sharp knives or razor blades
• fine-point markers, pencils
• construction paper
• scissors
• stamp pads (the more colors, the better)

On a piece of paper the same size as the flat, cut side of the potato, draw a design. With a knife or fine-point marker, trace the design onto the flat side of the potato. (If using numbers or letters, trace them backward on the potato so the letters or numbers will be the correct direction when printed.) The part of the design you cut out of the potato will be the color of your paper; the uncut part (or raised portion) of the potato will print in the color of ink you choose.

After the design is cut out, press the potato carefully onto the stamp pad, and then onto the paper, making a print. You can personalize stationery (for the group or individuals), membership cards, posters, or stickers. Print different colors of ink on top of each other, repeat the design as a border, or stamp a large sheet of paper and cover it with clear contact paper to use as a notebook folder, scrapbook cover, or book cover.

PUZZLE-PIECE MAILER

This little device is great for involving newcomers, making regulars feel special, and reaching out to inactive kids. The next time you have a special party or activity planned, buy a jigsaw puzzle and attach one piece to each invitation that you send. In the invitation, explain how each person has a unique contribution to make to the group, and that this piece represents his or her unique gift. Ask each person to bring the puzzle piece to the event in order to find out where it fits in the puzzle.

Not only does this kind of invitation serve as an attention-getter, it also encourages attendance. At the party itself, the puzzle becomes an icebreaker as people arrive with their pieces and are immediately welcomed and involved in putting the puzzle together.

PUZZLING PUBLICITY

Try this idea for turning a drab publicity flyer into an intellectual experience. Print a regular flyer, with lots of words and a cartoon or drawing. Take each flyer and cut it into puzzle pieces. For each puzzle, place the pieces in an envelope and mail it out. Be sure to include an instruction sheet. The kids have to put the pieces together in order to read the announcement.

It is best to cut each puzzle one at a time so the pieces won't get all mixed up and to ensure that every envelope has a complete announcement.

"REASONS WHY" MAILER

Here's a publicity idea that you may want to try sometime. Print up a mailer that folds in half. On the outside (front) of the card, print, "Good Reasons Why You Should *Not* Attend (such-and-such meeting)."

When you open up the card, the inside is blank. The details of the meeting are then printed on the back.

REVERSE ANNOUNCEMENTS

If you send out publicity notices regularly and get the impression that some of them are never read, here is an idea.

Photocopy your message onto a transparency; turn it over and place a white piece of paper behind the transparency, and copy it again. This copy will read from right to left and all the letters will be backward.

To read this, a kid will have to stand in front of a mirror. And if this extra effort is made, it practically guarantees your message will be read.

SCOREBOARD MAILER

Here's another letter idea to use when you mail out your youth schedule:

Dear Friends,

As a public service to you, your youth department is sending along the scores of this week's big games:
Union 76, Phillips 66
DC 10, Beverly Hills 90210
Boeing 747, Indianapolis 500

UB 40, V 8
U 2, Datsun 300
US 101, Route 66
Musketeers 3, Stooges 3 (tie)

You will really know the score if you join in on all the activities listed below. We'll be looking for you!

(List your youth schedule here.)

SCRAMBLED LETTER

One way to make sure your young people read every line of your next flyer is to send them a "scrambled" letter. First, type a draft of your letter and number the lines as you go. Next, type a final draft with all the lines scrambled. Include some instructions at the top. Here's an example (each line is numbered to show you which line to read next—start with Line 1 and go from there):

15 like us. Oh, and if you register early (by May 31), and attend all
 2 that we do things in very unconventional ways in Junior High Vacation
 5 ended up having fun. We do our own thing in our own room—even the
13 three-dimensional photo display for your room. It is real neat and
 8 and play volleyball, and eat (donuts, pizza, and other yummies). Some-
 1 You see, we have chosen this unusual letter to try to convince you
10 decide what). Of course, we have lessons too. That is the real meat
16 five days of VBS, you'll be eligible to win a cassette tape player.
12 even keeps the church mice listening in. Our craft this year is a

14 you can personalize it if you want. Try us—we think that you'll
 4 have attended Junior High VBS before. Some of the real grumps even
 7 little kids. We even do our own music. Plus . . . we go on field trips
 3 Bible School. If you don't believe us, just ask some of the kids who
 9 times we bowl, play miniature golf, or go to a state park (you can help
11 of VBS but Mark is not your ordinary boring, preacher-type. He
 6 missionary comes down to us instead of us sitting up with all the

Come join us,

Mark Matthews
Connie Flick
Connie Hamilton

THAT'S INCREDIBLE

    Here's a mailer or handout idea that your kids will love. The next time you print up a flyer or reminder for your group, list some incredible facts along with information on upcoming events. It could say something like:

All of the following are ABSOLUTELY, POSITIVELY true!

1. Wearing suspenders is illegal in Nogales, Arizona.
2. Forty percent of American adults cannot fill out a bank deposit slip correctly.
3. During a lifetime, the average American will eat 20,932 eggs and 8,200 pounds of potatoes.
4. The automatic transmission fluid in almost every car is whale oil.

5. The average adult has enough iron in his or her body to make a two-inch nail.
6. A Volkswagen Bug was compressed into a two-foot cube to serve as a coffee table for a Mahtomedi, Minnesota couple.
7. Rats are fastidiously clean. The expression "you dirty rat" slanders this furry pest. And rats are not mentioned in the Bible.
8. In Norton, Virginia, it's illegal to tickle a girl.
9. TNT* WILL BE AT LAUREN BUTLER'S HOUSE THIS WEEK, BEGINNING AT 7:01 p.m. SHARP. HERE'S A MAP THAT'S FACTUALLY CORRECT.

*Thursday Night Thing, where you get the facts of life . . . and more!

WANTED POSTER

Print up a supply of "wanted" posters for members of your group. On each poster, leave space for a personal touch, such as a cartoon characterization or a humorous photograph. If someone in your group has artistic ability, this can be a good project for him or her. These posters work great as mail-outs to youth program absentees. You can fill in ridiculous names such as "Dynamite Don" or "Insane Duane," and then write in what the absentee is wanted for, such as Sunday school, youth choir, or Bible study.

WARNING ANNOUNCEMENT

Plan to do back-to-back mailings. In the first mailing, send a postcard with the following warning: "Tomorrow you will receive a postcard. Read it." It is guaranteed that when you mail the second postcard the next day, people will be anxiously waiting for it.

Telephone Ideas

There are many ways to make the telephone work for your ministry promotion. These ideas can save you time and energy—and dramatically boost your ministry's effectiveness.

ANSWERING MACHINE HOTLINE

You can buy a telephone answering machine for as little as $70. Each week, record a new, creative message on the answering machine that highlights upcoming events and activities. Or, choose a wise saying from the book of Proverbs and record a parody of a popular TV program or commercial to communicate the proverb's message.

For example, you could record a parody of Robin Leach introducing "Lifestyles of the Rich and Famous" using Proverbs 23:4–5. At the end of your message, read the proverb and challenge callers to choose one way to help the poor this week.

Kids will become addicted to your weekly messages, and you can take advantage of their attention to communicate important information.

CALL-IN CONTEST

Publish a Bible trivia question in your youth newsletter. The first group member to call you or your answering machine with the correct answer wins a prize. Great prizes are contemporary Christian music cassettes or CDs, posters, T-shirts, food coupons, or even cash. This idea really works; just ask the disc jockeys at your local rock stations. To generate even more involvement and interest, move your Bible trivia question around in each newsletter.

FUN FONE

Make your answering machine into a Fun Fone. Offer contests of all kinds over the line. Get different people to read your message and ask the kids to "name the voice" for prizes.

Use random call-in awards. Whenever you change your message, invite the first caller to leave his or her name to receive a special prize. This keeps kids calling to see if they can get a chance to win. For example, offer a prize for the call closest to 11:00 a.m. on Wednesday. You'll have kids calling between classes or before lunch, and even parents will call, using their kids' names. It's fun, and everyone gets the message about an upcoming event.

Some phones have voice-mail systems that allow you to do broadcast dialing. Set up your phone lists and program them into a computer through a touch-tone phone. Record a message and let the computer call everyone in your youth group with an invitation to Sunday night's event. It's a quick way to make 30 or 300 calls in less than two minutes!

SING "HAPPY BIRTHDAY" OVER THE PHONE

If you have a computer at home or work, keep an up-to-date birthday list of all your kids on it. At the beginning of each day, check your list and treat your birthday guys or girls to your best rendition of "Happy Birthday" over the phone. Your kids will know that you care about them as individuals, not just as members of the group.

TELEPHONE BLITZ

This idea is far from new, but it works. It is simply a way to organize getting the word out to as many kids as possible.

Step 1:   Collect the names and phone numbers of as many kids as possible—old kids, new kids, anyone who is eligible to attend your meetings.

Step 2:   Appoint or elect a telephone chairperson. Choose someone who is a real go-getter and can motivate people. He or she is in charge of every telephone blitz. You'll also need to appoint or elect a transportation chairperson (see Step 6).

Step 3:   The telephone chairperson recruits callers who are responsible for calling up to ten people the evening before the meeting you're pushing. (If you have a list of one hundred people to call, you'll need ten callers.) The chairperson should give each caller his or her list of people to call at least two or three days in advance. Boys should get boys' names and girls should get girls.

Step 4:   On the day of the telephone blitz (usually the day before the meeting), the telephone chairperson calls his or her callers and reminds them to get going. The callers then call their ten people and invite them to tomorrow's meeting. Each caller should know the details of the meeting, such as time, place, what the program will be, and so on. If someone says he or she would like to come to the meeting, but doesn't have a ride, the caller should inform the person to be ready at a specific time and someone will come by and pick him or her up. Each caller should be prepared to answer questions.

Step 5:   After the callers have called all of the people on their lists, they report to the chairperson how many people are coming, not coming, not available, need rides, etc.

Step 6:   The telephone chairperson then calls the transportation chairperson who has lined up drivers to pick up people. The two chairpersons work out a plan for picking up people. The transportation chairperson then calls the available drivers and assigns them people who need rides.

NOTE: This procedure can be repeated every week before your youth meeting. This gets everybody involved and is extremely effective when carried out properly.

WELCOME-TO-OUR-GROUP TELEPHONE TEAM

Instead of sending visitors an impersonal form letter, why not train your kids to use the telephone to welcome them? Form a "Welcome-to-Our-Group" team of three or more kids. Train team members to telephone visitors to thank them for attending, to invite them to return, and to give them information about the youth group and upcoming activities.

Using Video

In the fall 1991 issue of *Youthworker Journal,* and in his delightful book *101 Things to Do with a Video Camera* (published by Gospel Light in 1988 and now out of print), Rick Bundschuh shared some valuable advice and offered practical ideas on how to give announcements using a video camera. Some of Rick's material is included in this chapter.

PEEP SHOW

Videotape ads for upcoming youth events. Rig up your video player and monitor in a box with a small peephole. Place the remote to run the video on top of the box. Because only one kid can see the show at a time, there will always be a line to see what is playing. Record the same message over and over so that everyone sees the same thing.

PLANNED COMMERCIALS

If your group takes an annual excursion to an amusement park, recreational area, or camp, think about next year's publicity while on this year's trip. Take along a video camera and videotape the group members on rides, eating, laughing, talking, and having fun.

Later in the year, when the event comes up again, edit and produce a number of short commercials for the trip. Show these commercials at several meetings or gatherings to remind everyone of the fun they had and to interest new members in signing up.

SORRY YOU'RE GONE

Send video messages to members of the group who have been sick or absent for awhile. Recruit some students to send the messages and give them some time to prepare. Their video notes can be either serious or goofy. Slip the finished cassette in the mail and brighten someone's day!

SPLICED ANNOUNCEMENTS

If you have more than one video recorder and a little bit of patience, you can create some hilarious announcements.

First, videotape your announcements. Next, use a video of an old slap-stick movie, and splice scenes from it into the tape of your announcements. (Make sure the films you use are in the public domain so you do not violate copyright laws.) You can use an old cops-and-robbers car chase scene in an announcement about a car rally. Or you can splice in a pie fight clip to announce a dessert event.

STRANGE ANNOUNCEMENTS

Go to various work environments and ask the people who work there if you could film them as they announce upcoming youth activities. For example, ask the trash collector to talk about camp as he empties your trash cans, or ask the cook at McDonald's to talk about the great food students will be served at the retreat.

THAT'S A MOUTHFUL

Record a staff person or a student making an announcement with a mouthful of gooey food. (Avocados work well because of their yucky green color.)

VIDEOCAM ON LOCATION

Pay a visit to the site of an upcoming camp or event. While there, make a promotional video using different locations at the site as settings. For example, at a camp you could say something like this, "Here we are at the top of Camp Bongo's fifty-foot slide to remind you of the great adventures awaiting you this summer!"

VOICE DUB

Videotape some big, tough guy making your announcement. Hold up a script off-camera for him to read. Afterward, dub in a girl's voice reading the same announcement. Kids will beg to hear the announcement again and again. By the way, don't tell the big guy what you're planning to do to him, and make sure that he's an understanding friend.

Announcements

A nd now for the announcements. . . .

Those words put most people to sleep. Wake up your group with creative announcements like the examples in this chapter.

ACTION ANNOUNCEMENTS

Here's a great way to put some life into announcement time, and to involve the kids in a creative way. Before the meeting begins, write out all the announcements that need to be made on slips of paper. Next, think of an unusual method of presenting each announcement. Try to choose a method that fits the particular announcement. Methods could be pantomime, poetry (turning the announcement into a rhyme), a news report, an interview, a song, alternating words (two individuals take turns reading every other word of the announcement), or charades. Also mark on each slip of paper the number of kids needed to make the announcement.

At the meeting, ask for volunteers. You don't have to tell them what they will be doing. It might be a good idea to match the methods and announcements with kids who will be able to pull it off. Send all the volunteers out of the room for five minutes or so to prepare their announcements while the group is singing or playing games. Have an adult sponsor go with them to offer suggestions. Call the volunteers back in and let them do their thing. You can even make a contest out of it, with the audience applauding for its favorite announcement.

Here's a sample of how an announcement slip might be written:

Pantomime—one person
Car wash
This Saturday at the church
10:00 a.m. to 4:00 p.m.

ALBUM ANNOUNCEMENT

To promote your group's activities, come up with a name for your group that sounds like a music group. Next, create a CD cover that looks like the real thing, complete with outrageous pictures of the "band"—the youth group leaders. There isn't a CD inside the case, but a calendar of the year's events and other information about your group's activities. If possible have the CD shrink-wrapped with plastic to look like a real CD. The kids will love it.

ANNOUNCEMENT CHARADES

If you always have lots of announcements to make, try this. Divide your group into teams of four or five kids. When the group is divided, give each team one or two announcements written on 3" x 5" cards. Each team has three minutes to come up with a charade of its announcement for the others to guess. Give a prize to the team with the most creative and effective charade. If all the announcements are about the same length and difficulty, divide into two teams and play a regular game of charades, timing the charades and awarding a prize to the fastest team. It's a sure-fire way of getting your kids involved in the announcements.

ANNOUNCEMENT CREATIONS

Do your young people having a hard time remembering upcoming events? You can strengthen their memories and have fun at the same time with this idea.

When it's announcement time at your next meeting, divide the group into teams and give each team an announcement, a piece of poster board, markers, and other supplies that might come in handy. In five minutes, each team must create an appealing announcement. It can be a poster, commercial, skit, song, cheer—anything team members want to create. Give an award to the group that does the best job.

With this approach, creativity is stimulated, the announcements are effective, and the kids are less likely to forget what's happening.

ANNOUNCEMENT TREASURE HUNT

If your announcements are sometimes forgotten or ignored, try an announcement treasure hunt.

Divide the group into small hunting teams. Give each team a 3" x 5" card with one or more facts about the upcoming event, as well as a clue that reveals where it will find the next card.

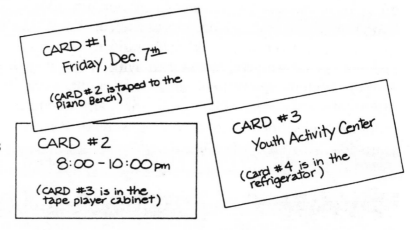

CARD #1
Friday, Dec. 7th

(CARD #2 is taped to the Piano Bench)

CARD #2
8:00 - 10:00 pm

(CARD #3 is in the tape player cabinet)

CARD #3
Youth Activity Center

(Card #4 is in the refrigerator)

You'll need a different set of cards with a different announcement for each team. When each team has found all its cards, team members arrange the facts in the proper order and make the announcement to the rest of the group.

This game can also be done as a relay, with one person from each team chasing down the clue cards and returning to the group. It adds a lot of fun and excitement to announcements and helps fight those age-old excuses of "I forgot" and "I didn't know about that."

Great Promotion and Publicity Ideas for Youth Ministry

CANDY ANNOUNCEMENTS

Tape candy to flyers, and then throw them out to the students.

COMPANIONS FLY FREE

Announce to your kids that if they bring a friend to a paid activity, their friends get to attend the activity free.

COSTUMED ANNOUNCEMENTS

For a change of pace, dress up a high schooler in an ice hockey goalie's uniform, military uniform, or some other outfit or costume to make the announcement.

DINNER THEATER ANNOUNCEMENTS

Here are three promotional skits that were used to promote a Valentine's Day youth group dinner theater. You can adapt the skits to fit your own February special occasion. Be sure to clear the skit with your supervisors, and make sure there's plenty of time to perform the skit during your church's regular services.

Skit One

Mr. and Mrs. Loud, a couple who not only talk loudly but also dress loudly, are dressed in clashing polyester outfits. Mr. Loud's hair is slicked down, and Mrs. Loud wears a flowered hat and cat's-eye glasses—reminiscent of how the Beverly Hillbillies might dress for a fancy occasion. Both speak in a very loud drawl. The couple enter the sanctuary late, and walk down the center aisle to the front. There, they turn to face the congregation and continue talking very loudly to each other.

He (*yelling*): Let's sit back here in case the preacher sprays when he preaches—I forgot my handkerchief today.

She (*in an equally loud voice*): Mr. Loud, how many times do I have to tell you that I like being up front? I want to hear the choir. If they aren't too good, maybe we'll join. I'd like to wear one of them purty robes. Besides, if the preacher's a sprayer, I'll give you some Kleenex. (*Pulls out a Kleenex, blows her nose loudly, filling the Kleenex—which she hands to Mr. Loud*)

He: This shur is a big fancy church. (*Fumbles with the bulletin, and sends inserts flying.*) Look how much stuff is in their bulletin. I like this church. Now, I'll always have paper to doodle on during the preachin'!

She: Let me see that. Wow, they even got colored paper in here! Look at this (*reading slowly and with difficulty*), "Student ministries presents"— that must be a fancy name for a youth group—"Student ministries presents the Calvary Dinner Theater, 6:45 to 9:30, February 14 and 16." That's on Valentine's Day and the Saturday after, ain't it? (*Continues reading*) "Tickets, $9.50 per person."

He: I spend more than that at Baker's Square!

She: Yeah, but you eat half a pie for dessert.

He: Well, you eat the other half.

She *(continuing to read, loudly and laboriously)*: "Please join us for an evening of cul . . . culi . . . cauliflower . . . no, that ain't it . . . cul-i-na-ry delight and thee-at-rical merriment."

He: What does that mean?

She: It means there'll be skits and stuff after the dinner. *(Slowly sounding out the syllables)* "An impeccable evening to venerate your Valentine sentiments."

He: They gonna venerate their Valentine sentiments right here at church???

She *(hitting him with her purse)*: I'll venerate my Valentine sentiments!

He: Does it say what they're gonna eat?

She *(reading)*: "Le Menu, Poulet Grille."

He: That must be the cook—Paulette Griller.

She: "Rits me-lanj, harry cots verts ox champ . . . champ-pig-nons."

He: What is that stuff?

She: I don't know what this harry cots is, but I think they're gonna serve a champion pig.

He: Oh, boy!

She: "For reservations, please call 282-2612, or put a check into the offering plate."

He: They always want a check in the offering plate.

She: Honey, can we go to this here dinner theater?

He: Why, sure, Sugar Lumpkins.

She: Oh, there's even sumthin' here about what to wear. *(Reading)* "Dress code: Please dress as ostentashuslee and as gawdilee as possible. Put on those ties, prom dresses, and costume jewelry. Sequins are a welcome sight."

He *(as the two walk back down the aisle)*: I just hope we have something to wear. It's so hard to be ostentashus.

Skit Two

Mr. and Mrs. Megabucks are expensively dressed. Mr. Megabucks could have a hat and cane, plus an unlit pipe in his mouth. Mrs. Megabucks could have a sequined purse, a fur, hat, white gloves, and lots of costume jewelry. Their speech should be distinct, loud, and haughty. (Think of Mr. and Mrs. Thurston Howell III from *Gilligan's Island.*) Ham it up. The two enter talking and walk down the center aisle to the front of the sanctuary and stand behind a microphone.

She: It's really so difficult to find a church worthy of our attendance.

He: I know exactly what you mean, my dear. Not a single BMW or Porsche in the parking lot. But there were certainly a lot of those . . .

Both *(disdainfully, in unison)*: Minivans!

She: Furthermore, I was disappointed with the doorman. Far too friendly. I like my help to be seen, not heard. They really should purchase uniforms for those people. Those little badges they wear that say "Greeter" on them give me a dreadful feeling of equality with the hired help.

He: The absence of a valet service certainly strikes two points against our coming here.

She: Yes, it was appalling to have to walk in from the parking lot.

He *(perusing the bulletin and inserts)*: As I examine this newsletter, I fail to notice any mention of a men's polo club or even a racquetball club.

She: Darling, you don't play racquetball, and you're allergic to horses.

He: Not the point, my dear. The lack of these two very fine forms of entertainment only emphasizes the absence of elegance—an absence that violates our sense of refinement. Not to mention that attending this church would certainly diminish our social status.

She: There does appear to be one exception, darling. Hand me that colored insert. *(Reading)* "Student ministries presents the Calvary Dinner Theater."

He: Now, that sounds like a prestigious group.

She: Yes, and it appears that they're holding a truly cultural event. Listen to this, "The dinner is to be on the evenings of February 14 and 16. Tickets are only $9.50."

He: Excellent planning. We can justify the expenditure as an investment in our love.

She: How romantic! *(Continues reading)* "Please join us for an evening of culinary delight and theatrical merriment."

He: By Jove, I could use some culinary delight—and I certainly enjoy the theater. I wonder if they'll be doing Shakespeare?

She: Oh, wouldn't that be grand? Listen to this, darling: "An impeccable evening to venerate your Valentine sentiments."

He: The very words I was thinking, my dear.

She: And the food sounds absolutely divine.

He: Read the menu, my dear.

She: I can't. It's in French.

He: In French! Simply elegant!

She: And look, they've even put in a dress code for the commoners.

He: Very open-minded of that student ministries group. I find myself actually eager to mix some with the lower classes.

She: This church may keep us from the horrible arrogance that is so-o-o prevalent in our world today.

He: Thank God, we're not snobs, my dear. *(Both exit.)*

Skit Three

Iam Lonely, an unsuccessful dating specialist, is a nerd and looks it, complete with taped glasses, untucked white shirt, mussed hair, a plethora of pens in his pockets, and flood pants. A leader or a student introduces Iam with words to this effect: "This morning, we have a special announcement from dating specialist, Iam Lonely."

Iam (*awkwardly, nervously approaches the microphone, stumbles as he reaches it and almost knocks it over*): One, two, three . . . testing . . . one, two, three . . . is this thing working? It is? Oh, good. My name is Iam Lonely, the world's foremost authority on first dates. I have had more first dates than anyone on earth. Unfortunately, I never have any second dates.

Many of you think going to a movie is a good first date. Incorrect. First of all, the popcorn is far too expensive. Second, your date may compare you with the actors on the screen and drop you like a hot potato. *(Defensively.)* Now, don't think that this has ever happened to me personally, but, uh, it has happened to some of my closest friends.

Others prefer to go bowling on their first date. The bowling alley, however, is not a good place to strike the match of love either. Reason number one: You may embarrass yourself with a low score. This has not been my problem; I have a 68-pin average. Reason number two: Your date may be embarrassed. I believe this is the case with many of my dates. For some reason, they never want to be seen with me in public. I've concluded that this is due to their poor bowling skills. Reason number three: Your thumb may become lodged in the ball and you may find yourself sliding down the alley right into the pins. This sporting moment is not a pleasant one; although when this very event transpired on a recent first date, my ball and I scored a strike. Nevertheless, I contend that those who go bowling for a first date are headed straight for the gutter.

"So," you ask, "what is a good first date?" I'm glad you asked. Please locate the colored insert in your bulletin. It gives you the details of not only the best first date, but, and I'm speaking to those who have already articulated your nuptial vows, the best evening to rekindle the romance in your marriages.

Please read this carefully with me:

(Reads)"Student ministries presents the Calvary Dinner Theater." A dinner theater is an appropriate dating environment. It provides one with ample opportunity for conversation, as well as entertaining diversions for those times when one lacks subject matter to discuss.

(Continues reading) "6:45 p.m. to 9:30 p.m., February 14 and 16." That is this Thursday and Saturday. Another reason to commend the dinner theater for your first date is that I have found it's always a good idea to have a second alternative to your initial request. By the time your potential date thinks of an excuse not to go with you on Thursday, you can spring Saturday on her. Because it is difficult to think of two legitimate excuses within 30 seconds, you'll probably snag your potential date for one of those evenings.

"Tickets are $9.50 per person." This is a genuine bargain. A movie and McDonald's (a terrible first date, by the way), approaches over $10 per person—even if you go dutch, which I recommend for first dates. No sense investing in a possible dead-end relationship. The dinner theater price of $9.50 per ticket is far less than I had to pay for the repair of the bowling alley lane.

I trust you will read for yourself the descriptions about the food and entertainment.

Note especially the bottom of the insert, which explains how to make reservations: "For reservations please call 828-4261." That's the church office number. When you call, a very pleasant receptionist will ask you for the information that you see on the bottom of your insert. Please do not ask out the receptionist. She is married, a startling fact in view of her ignoring my first-date advice.

Another method of registering is to simply fill out the form you are now looking at and turn it in to the office, or place it in the offering plate.

Finally, I would like to say a word about blind dates. I have found that blind dates are one of the most effective ways to get a date. I myself am nearsighted, an impairment that helps conversation inestimably. Just be careful not to step on your date's cat.

That's all the advice for today. Make your reservations soon—and happy dating.

EXCUSE ME

Advertising an event? First, make a list of every excuse students could possibly give for not attending the event. Next, blow up a balloon for each excuse. Tie a string to each balloon too. During your plug for the event, hold the handful of balloons by their strings. Pop a balloon and read one of the excuses on the list. End the announcement with something like this, "If you don't come, you'll burst my bubble."

FOOD FUN ANNOUNCEMENT

Have one person stand in front of the group and announce the details of the event. Meanwhile, two other people keep reappearing, and very methodically and calmly smash things such as eggs, spinach, a banana (in the ear), flour, and chocolate syrup on the announcer. When the last item is smashed, the announcer (who has remained deadpan up to this point), pulls out an inflatable plastic club from behind his or her back and whacks the bothersome people. The effect is hilarious, and it really gets peoples' attention. (Have the announcer stand on a disposable plastic dropcloth for this one!)

FREE TICKET

Next time you plan a party or special meeting in which you would like to draw a good crowd, print up "free" tickets that can be used the same way as handouts. Psychologically, tickets have a lot more drawing power than normal handouts or announcements. Even though you aren't charging anything to come in the first place, people think they really have something valuable when they have complimentary tickets.

Include all the details of your event on the ticket. For the best results, either have your information typeset by a printing company, or have an artist hand-letter the information in an attractive way.

GIANT TICKET

A good way to both announce and create a lot of talk about an event is to print up "giant" tickets. This is especially effective when an admission fee is being charged. The results of this kind of promotion are as follows:

- Kids will not only want to buy a ticket for the event, but they will also want to buy the ticket just to get the ticket. It promotes ticket sales.
- It creates an unusual image for your event. Because the ticket is unusual, the event will probably be different too.
- Kids will talk about it. "Hey, did you buy one of those wild tickets?"

- The ticket makes a good souvenir after the event. A kid brings it to the event for admission, you punch a hole in it or stamp it, and return it to the kid. He or she can hang it on his or her bedroom wall as a reminder of how much fun he or she had.

The giant ticket can be printed at a very low cost. It should be done in two different ink colors—a bright fluorescent color and black. Print the ticket on heavy paper stock. The important thing is that the ticket should look sharp, and the bigger the better. Youth Specialties once used a giant ticket for a film showing at Universal City Studios in Hollywood. The really wild thing was seeing two hundred youth directors show up with these huge fluorescent tickets. And because everyone had something in common (a giant ticket), it helped people to laugh and talk even though they had never met. A giant ticket is especially good to promote banquets, graduation parties, and other events where people have a tendency to be extra proper and formal.

HOW TO EVADE A DATE

Announce your next youth event with the following skit. Irwin calls Susan for a date. He is nervous and awkward during the conversation, but he's determined to get a date. Susan, desperate for reasons to refuse, uses the youth group calendar for convenient excuses—each excuse, of course, being an actual announcement of an upcoming event for your group. Replace Susan's excuses with your own group's upcoming events. As usual, ham it up to add to the fun.

You'll need three volunteers for the narrator, Irwin, and Susan. For props, you'll need two telephones, a trash can, and a crumpled copy of the youth calendar of events.

Setting: **Irwin,** stage left, is nervously pacing. **Susan,** chewing gum and wearing a cheerleader's outfit, stands with her back to the audience at stage right.

Narrator: February has begun, and within this auspicious month lurks a holiday that puts us all in the mood for love. Yes, I'm talking about President's Day—I mean, Valentine's Day. While we all enjoy the thought of romance, you probably don't go out with just anyone who calls. As a service to those of you who must plot ways of getting out of a date, we now present to you a brief educational drama called, "How to Evade a Date."

Irwin *(nervously rubbing his palms together as he works up courage to make a phone call)*: Eight-three-one-four-five-seven-eight. One ring, two ri— Hello? This is Irwin. Do you want to go out with me this Friday night? Oh … sorry, Mr. Vanity . . . uh, is Irwin there? I mean, is Miss Susan Vanity there? … Yes sir, I'll hold.

Susan *(enters calling over her shoulder in a sickeningly sweet voice)*: Okay, Daddy. I'll get it on my own phone. *(Picks up receiver)* Hello?

Irwin: Hello. Is this Susan Vanity?

Susan: Yes.

Irwin: Hi, Susan. This is Irwin Test-Tube. I'm in your biology class.

Susan *(obviously not recognizing Irwin's voice)*: Yes?

Irwin: I sit right in front of you… *(awkward pause)*… you copy my answers during tests.

Susan *(nervously clearing her throat)* Yes, I know who you are now.

Irwin: Well, I was wondering, Susan, if you'd like to go to a movie with me this Friday night? "Return of the Dead" is showing at the Cinemax for only a dollar.

Susan: Oh, I'd love to, Irwin, but I have to... to... *(looks frantically around her room, sees the trash can, reaches in, and pulls out a crumpled copy of the youth group calendar)*... I have to go to a junior high progressive dinner with my church. It starts at six and goes until almost midnight. But it would have really been fun. Sorry, but—

Irwin: But you're in high school.

Susan: I know, Irwin, but I promised to... uh... help with the dishes.

Irwin: How about joining me on Saturday, February 24? There's a really swell exhibit at the science museum on the reproductive rituals of African elephants.

Susan: Well, that does sound interesting, but I... *(still scanning the calendar)* ... I'll be gone the entire weekend on a retreat in northern Minnesota with my youth group—you know, skiing, horseback riding, playing broomball, cheering the snow football players.

Irwin: Well, what about Wednesday, the 14th? I hear there's an Elvis look-alike contest at the mall.

Susan: Sorry. Gotta go to church and make sure I pay my deposit for the retreat by that night. And every Wednesday I have youth group.

Irwin: How about Tuesday?

Susan: Uh, Tuesdays... no, I use Tuesdays to wash my hair so I look good for

---

youth group.

Irwin: Sunday night?

Susan: No good. Small groups at—

Susan and Irwin *(in unison)*: church.

Irwin: How does March look?

Susan: Well, I don't have that calendar yet, but I know that there is a junior high retreat I'll need to pray for and a high school progressive dinner on the seventeenth. Boy, I'm afraid I'm pretty booked up.

Irwin: You know, all that stuff is beginning to sound fun. Maybe I can come with you to some of them?

Susan: Sorry, Irwin, I've got to go. I hear your mother calling. Bye, and thanks for calling. *(Hangs up)*

Irwin *(looking at phone)*: Boy, is she ever religious. And I wonder why my mother was calling her?

The End *(Massive applause)*

LIP-SYNC ANNOUNCEMENT

Play a cassette recording of the announcement as the announcement-giver lip syncs it. With practice, she can mouth the words just enough out of sync with the recording so it looks even more strange, sort of like a poorly dubbed foreign film.

LOOKING UP

If you have a difficult time getting your youth group to listen to announcements, here's a way to get their attention. Thumb tack or tape your announcements or posters to the ceiling. Remember to print them large enough to read. You can put the posters or announcements anywhere—in the hallways, youth room, or wherever kids congregate. Once someone starts looking up, pretty soon the whole group will.

PIZZA DELIVERY

Is the announcement for your adult congregation? Dress up a high schooler like a pizza delivery person, and have him or her run up to the pulpit during announcements with a pizza for the pastor. When the "delivery" person suddenly realizes what church this is, he or she asks the pastor why he's ordering out for pizza when his own youth group is taking orders for a fund-raising pizza sale. By the way, make arrangements with your pastor first.

POSTER PROJECTIONS

For a quick, inexpensive way to get the word out about an event or activity, use an overhead projector to project your poster on an entire wall. It's cheaper than posters, and you can utilize a whole wall. If you or your youth are not exceptionally talented when it comes to art, it's a breeze to trace

lettering and pictures with a clear transparency.

PUZZLED ANNOUNCEMENTS

If announcements have been a drag in your meeting, try this. Think up various kinds of word puzzles whose answers are the details of coming events. Many types of puzzles will work—crossword puzzles, word searches, or even logic puzzles. Make copies of the puzzle and pass them out at the end of the meeting. Kids will need to figure out the puzzle to know what is coming up. Post a completed puzzle later on just in case no one solves it.

SIGN-UP SHEETS

Tape sign-up sheets under all the seats. Attach a dollar bill to one or two of the sheets. Or attach stickers to a couple of sign-up sheets. Sticker holders may go to the front and claim a prize.

VANISHING OPPORTUNITY

As you make an announcement, hold up a piece of paper with the same announcement written on it in big, bold letters. End your spiel by saying something like, "And don't forget to sign up next Sunday. After that, your opportunity to attend this event will be gone." At this point, pull a lighter from your pocket and ignite the sheet of paper, tossing it into the air as you do. The paper will flame up and totally disappear in a flash.

The trick is to use "flash paper" that you can buy in a magic or novelty shop. Don't try it with regular paper or you're liable to burn down the church. Flash paper is safe and grabs the kids' attention.

VISUAL REMINDERS

During busy seasons when you have several events to promote (such as December or the summer), bring a bagful of items to visually remind your group of the events. For example, pull out of your bag a combination lock for lock-ins, ski goggles for a ski trip, a Christmas ornament for a Christmas party, a cassette tape or CD for a Christian concert, and a hammer for a service project. The second week you announce these events, all you'll have to do is pull the appropriate objects from the bag (Santa's bag, if it's December), and the kids will shout out the events.

WILD PITCH

Here's a good way to advertise the beginning of your church's softball season or any other event that you want to advertise with a baseball theme. Cut a baseball in half with a power saw, then attach one half of the baseball to one side of a pane of glass in a window, and the other half to the other side, so it looks as if the ball is stuck in the window. Ideally, the window should be located in a high-traffic area of the church. You can also paint some "cracks" around the ball to make it look more authentic.

Under the ball, post your announcement, sign-up list, or whatever. With a little creativity, you can use this attention-getter for all kinds of announcements: a "spring training" seminar, a sales "pitch," or a good way to have a "ball."

YOUTH GROUP ANNUAL

Begin a youth group Annual. Have someone take pictures at all of your group happenings. Someone else can report newsworthy items to your local newspaper, and if any of the items are published, he or she can clip out these articles for the Annual. You'll need a three-ring binder and some acetate-covered sheets for mounting the articles and pictures.

The Annual can be used to advertise coming events as well as provide your youth group members with good memories of fun times. Include the names of your youth group officers, retreat committee, sponsors, and anyone who has received any special recognition for anything.

Newsletters

chapter 11

Newsletters can be fun to put together and enjoyable to read. They can add life to a dead group, and involve a lot of students.

Here are some creative ideas you can use to spice up your newsletters:

CLIP-OUT COUPONS

Include clip-out coupons that serve a dual purpose. The coupons announce upcoming activities, and give kids discounts on those activities. Kids are motivated to read the announcements because they'll save money.

CRAZY CAPERS

To liven up your newsletter, just slip in a few phony events. Among all the straight stuff, insert an event that is so ridiculous that it would be impossible to do, but might fake out someone for a few seconds when he or she first reads it. If nothing else, it will cause kids to pay more attention to your communications. These phony events can add some spark and enthusiasm to your group as kids anticipate your next crazy caper.

Here are a couple of examples:

Sunday, June 31: Overnight Field Trip to Iceberg, Texas. Tour of the petrified Iceberg Museum. Leave church at 12 noon and return when gas is available. Bring one VISA card and all the enemies you want.

Saturday, August 18.5: Skydiving in Hines Park. Bring chute (or reinforced umbrella) and a sack lunch. Meet at church (for prayer). Transportation provided by Schrader's Funeral Home and Traffic Copter #95—we're ready when you are.

GRAMS

Create a "Grams" column for kids to send quick messages to each other in the newsletter.

NEWSLETTER PRIZES

Do you wonder if your newsletter gets read thoroughly? If you have your doubts, try including a contest that requires kids to report important facts from the newsletter to you. For example, print that the person who is the fifteenth caller to a certain number after 3:30 p.m. on Monday, October 18 wins a pizza, a CD, concert tickets, or another prize.

Each caller must also answer several questions about the activities that were announced in your newsletter. Many kids will read the entire newsletter for the answers and call in. The better the prize, the better your newsletter will be read!

NEWSLETTER SEARCH

If your young people tend to take the newsletter for granted, try this. Announce that you plan to distribute the next newsletter differently to save on postage. Tell kids to bring a flashlight to the next meeting.

Before that meeting, address all your newsletters as usual, but instead of mailing them, hide the newsletters all over the church. Put them in hard-to-find places, but keep track of where each person's newsletter is. When the kids arrive, instruct them to search the church for their own copies of the newsletter. If a kid finds someone else's newsletter, he or she must leave it where it is.

Give prizes to the first few people who find their newsletters, and booby prizes to those who are last or who fail to find them at all. Following the search, read the newsletter together and emphasize important items.

NEWSLETTERS TO PARENTS OF TEENS

Newsletters designed specifically for parents are the best tools for keeping them informed. Be careful not to send newsletters too often, or they won't be read. Church bulletins are a good means of communication too.

In your communication, let parents know the reason behind your plans—why you are doing what you are doing. The parent who is concerned with spiritual content needs to know that it is important for kids to have fun together once in a while. Send a letter to parents each spring, explaining why summer camp is a vital experience for kids. It's important that parents understand your reasoning behind what you're attempting to do and teach.

Calendars

chapter

12

C alendars can be one of the most effective and cost-efficient means to promote your ministry. They can inform, entertain, and motivate your kids and their parents to participate in your activities.

CALENDAR WATER BOTTLE

Quench your kids' thirst for summertime activities by printing your summer calendar on water bottles (or sport bottles). Print whatever you usually print on a calendar—names and times of programs, parties, retreats, studies—on the bottles. Add some colorful graphics (coordinated with the colors of the bottle and lid), include your youth group name, and then make the bottles available to visitors as well as regulars at the beginning of your summer program.

A few phone calls to printers in your area will get you started on how to print on the water bottles. Otherwise, contact Countryside Products, Box 13256, Columbus, OH 43213, 614-861-6116.

CANNED PUBLICITY

Here's a different annual or seasonal calendar idea. Print the calendars so they look like can labels, and then stick them on real tin cans. You can purchase empty cans from a local packing plant for a nominal cost. If you can get cans with removable lids, then the cans can double as banks for saving money for the events.

Stack all the cans in your meeting room as if they're on a grocery store shelf, and then hand out the cans to all the kids. Chances are the cans won't get lost like so many other announcements that kids take home.

FREE BROCHURES

Next time you're planning a yearly or seasonal calendar mailing to members of your group, contact the places you'll be patronizing for free brochures. Amusement parks, recreation areas, cities and towns, campgrounds, restaurants, or hotels often print up attractive, colorful brochures that you can include with your calendar to generate excitement and interest.

GIANT CALENDAR POSTER

A great way to keep your youth group aware of coming activities is to print giant calendars on brightly colored paper, with each activity listed in its appropriate place. The calendars make great wall hangings and are a constant reminder that something is going on all the time. Check your local print shop for prices and available paper stocks.

HEAD-FOR-THE-SUMMER CALENDAR

Members of one youth group put their heads together about how to publicize their summer program—and decided that their heads were the very place for it! Call silk-screen printers who print T-shirts, and ask if they also print on painters' caps. (Most do. If no one does locally, call American Mills in Minneapolis for prices and a catalog, 1-800-876-4287.)

Once you get a reasonable quote, use a laser printer and print out your summer schedule. Take the printout, plus a copy of your youth group's logo and some clip art to the screen printer. These painter's caps printed with your group's logo and summer schedule make great publicity—and kids love wearing them during the summer too.

POCKET CALENDAR

Design a brightly colored pocket calendar with all the upcoming dates of both church and youth activities. It helps prevent a lot of church programming conflicts and keeps kids, youth advisors, and parents posted on what's going on.

SHRINKING CALENDAR

Want to keep your teenagers' parents informed of upcoming activities, especially those that require parental permission? Print up a calendar for each kid with different detailed announcements about the events. On the back, print a parental permission form for each announcement. Position the form back-to-back with the corresponding announcement on the front.

Have group members take their calendars home and hang them up in their rooms. When it's time for an activity, a young person can cut out that section from the calendar, ask a parent to fill out the form on the back, and turn it in. The calendar grows smaller as each activity is cut out.

SPIRAL CALENDAR

The shape isn't the only unusual feature about this monthly or quarterly activity calendar. Between the events, include whimsical one-liners that mention the names of the kids in the group.

To make this kind of calendar, draw fifteen or so concentric circles. Start filling in the outermost circle, and then erase a segment of the circle to form a "gateway" to the next circle. Do this for all the circles.

The calendar's effect is dizzying, but kids will read it to the end, if for no other reason than to catch all the quips and see if their names are mentioned. Also, with some clever scissors work, kids can make mobiles to hang in their rooms.

TV GUIDE ANNOUNCEMENT

Here's another variation on a calendar that works great. Print a booklet that looks like the *TV Guide* or your local TV listings publication. List all of your activities and meetings for each month like TV shows. A little creative writing and a sense of humor will make this idea a winner with your kids.

YOUTH GROUP COUPON BOOK

Here's an alternative to the annual youth group calendar. Print up a coupon book with coupons for every event of the year. Some of the coupons can simply be announcements for the events, but others can be actual discount coupons for camp registration or retreat deposits. For certain events, include extra coupons that can be given to friends. Design the booklet to look like the real thing, using clip art and fancy borders.

Posters and Bulletin Boards

chapter
13

I was involved with teenagers in one church when I realized that many of them attended Sunday school but not church, or vice versa. This meant there were kids who didn't hear about teen activities. To remedy this situation, we started using posters and bulletin boards. They were enjoyable to and ensured that everyone found out about upcoming events, regardless of which class or service they attended. Enthusiasm grew for the activities, not only among the teens, but also among their parents.

BILLBOARD POSTERS

Make a billboard-size poster. If you explain your purpose (communicating youth group events) to an outdoor advertising company, the people in charge may be happy to give you old billboard posters free. These posters come in sheets of heavy paper about 5' x 8' and are great for making giant posters. This kind of poster making can be fun for your group, so provide plenty of floor space, big paint brushes, and water-base paint; then let your kids be as creative as they want.

BOX BULLETIN BOARD

Collect a few shoe boxes. For each box, make a hole in one end (large enough to see into the box) and a slit in the lid for light. Place announcements and photos on the inside of the box, opposite the peek hole. Attach the boxes at eye level to the youth bulletin board. The uniqueness of the boxes will attract many who would ordinarily ignore the bulletin board. To attract even more attention to the bulletin board, vary the size of the boxes.

BULLETIN BOARD ON WHEELS

The youth room in most churches is not located near the main foyer—it's usually hidden and out of the way. Therefore, the publicity in your youth room doesn't reach most kids and adults.

A bulletin board on wheels gets your publicity where the people are. You can roll the board to the main hall on Sundays and to a meeting room on weeknights. Make your bulletin board colorful and attractive, and take it to where the people are!

If you have trouble getting kids to read the news and announcements posted on the youth group bulletin board, try this. Have someone shoot photos at all of your youth activities, and each week hang a new batch of pictures on the board. Appropriate humorous captions can be placed under each photo for added fun. Kids love to see themselves and their friends, and they'll make it a point to check out the bulletin board every week.

BULLETIN BOARD TREE

If bulletin board space is at a premium, build a bulletin board tree on which you can hang several announcements at a time. (See the illustration at right.) If the bulletin board is portable, you can cart it around to all your group functions. Hang up a few humorous things on occasion (cartoons, crazy pictures, etc.), and kids will check out the tree whenever they see it.

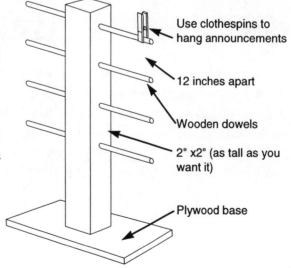

Use clothespins to hang announcements

12 inches apart

Wooden dowels

2" x2" (as tall as you want it)

Plywood base

COVER YOUR BULLETIN BOARD

Before putting anything on your bulletin board, cover it with burlap or other suitable material. This will enhance the appearance, because you won't be able to detect unsightly pin or nail holes. Don't use a color of material that will interfere with whatever you put on the board. An antique green or blue are two suitable background colors.

CREATIVE GUNNY SACKS

Burlap gunny sacks make interesting and attractive murals, bulletin boards, or pictures. All you do is mount the gunny sack on the bulletin board, and paint your message with oil paint or thick poster paint, or use wide-tip markers. The results are usually very effective.

CREATIVE LIGHTING

Think about how you'll use lighting with your bulletin board. Unless you have a specific purpose for low lighting, you should have good bright lighting. If necessary, shield any lights to prevent a glare on the board. This will also focus the light to shine directly on your bulletin board. Use blinking lights, moving objects, three-dimensional figures, and bright colors to draw attention to your bulletin board—just be sure the message doesn't get lost.

DIFFERENT-SIZED BOXES

Boxes of different sizes in good condition can also add an interesting design element for your bulletin board. You may want to spray paint the boxes to make them more attractive. Put the open end of the box against the bulletin board, and use the bottom of the box for information or photos.

DROP CLOTH DISPLAY

A painter's canvas drop cloth provides an excellent and inexpensive portable wall and background for a promotional message that you'll want to use again and again. Ask at your local paint store or art store for the best type of paint to use on the drop cloth; then create away. You can bring out the wall whenever and wherever it's needed, and neatly store it away until you're ready to use it again.

DRY-ERASE CALENDAR BOARD

Here's how to make a monthly calendar bulletin board that's as fun to create as it is to look at.

You'll need a large dry-erase white board. Purchase black pinstriping from an auto parts store. Use the striping to divide the board into thirty-five squares, like a calendar—seven across and five down.

Use different colors of dry-ink pens to write in the dates and events that you've planned for the month. Attach clip art, photos, and other stuff to make the board colorful and interesting. Use your imagination.

Place the board where everyone can see it, including parents. It will attract a lot of attention, and because it's erasable, you can use it over and over again.

FREE CAR

On a poster, in large letters, write, "FREE CAR AT YOUTH CLUB." Write one word per line and leave plenty of space between the words. In smaller letters, above the word "FREE," write the word "Feel." Between the words "FREE" and "CAR," write in smaller letters, "to come by." Between the word "CAR" and the words "AT YOUTH CLUB," in smaller letters write, "to a terrific program." Your final message will read, "Feel FREE to come by CAR to a terrific program AT YOUTH CLUB".

You can use this technique for any message. Here's another example.

In large letters, write "LAST MEETING." In smaller letters above it, write "If you thought our." In smaller letters below it, write "was good wait till you come to the next one."

MOVABLE OBJECTS

Three-dimensional objects, springs, or even sections of hoses can be used on a bulletin board to enhance and attract attention to it. Often you can pick up a variety of objects at a supermarket for free. You will find many businesses are very cooperative about donating materials. I once went to an ice cream shop that had several pictures of sundaes, sodas, milk shakes, and banana splits. I asked if I could have them, and the people in charge even gave me a small turntable that I used for a fake sundae made out of plaster.

PEEP BOX

This idea is a great way to get kids to read bulletin board information. Build a big box out of plywood that is about 3' wide by 3' deep by 3' high. Mount the box on legs and cut a hole in the bottom of the box just big enough for a kid to stick his or her head through. Paint the outside of the box or decorate it in some creative way. One side of the box should be hinged, so that it can open and then be locked shut. To light up the inside of the box, use a small light bulb of some kind (battery operated, perhaps). On all four inside walls of the box, hang your posters, announcements, pictures, and other items of interest. Kids have to crawl under the box and poke their heads up through the hole to see what is inside. If you have time, change the contents of the box every week. Soon kids will stand in line to see what is inside, just to satisfy their curiosity. And these are the same kids who would ignore a traditional bulletin board.

For a variation of this idea, use a black light inside the box, and write all of your signs and announcements with fluorescent markers or paints. The effect is fascinating.

A way to get good use out of your peep box is to place it in a strategic location where a lot of kids pass by, such as a popular hangout or on a school campus itself or somewhere near the school where a lot of kids walk by. The box is a great way to advertise upcoming youth events—as long as you make the box's contents as interesting as possible.

PHOTO ENDORSEMENTS

Do you routinely take pictures of your students at various get-togethers? If you don't, start the habit now. A supply of pictures is a good resource for publicity. Here's an example. When you want to publicize an event, select and mount some pictures of teens in your group.

Next, draw, on white paper, comic strip-style speech bubbles. Think up entertaining and informative dialogue about the upcoming events to put in the speech bubbles. Cut out the speech bubbles and glue them next to the teens in the photos. Make the dialogue fun, but not embarrassing to anyone. If you think the photos might be torn down, mount them inside a large glass poster frame.

POSTER SHOTS

Many local photo processors can now convert your photos to posters, stickers, or puzzles. Consult the yellow pages under "Photo Finishing" for options.

REFRIGERATOR BOX

Refrigerator or appliance boxes make great portable advertisements. Post flyers, promotional ads, and sign-up sheets on all four sides, and stand the box up in a conspicuous place.

You can also cut peepholes in the box's side. Write, "LOOK!" in large letters near the holes. Peoples' curiosity won't let them go by without checking inside. On the inside, tack flyers and other bulletin board items. Either leave the top open or use a light bulb to keep everything visible inside.

SCHIZO PORTRAITS

Take everyone's picture with a Polaroid camera. To take the shot, use a plain background and make sure each person is the same distance from the camera and centered (not off to the right or left), looking straight ahead. When all the photos are developed, cut each picture in half, right under the eyes, straight across. Then match each person's top half to someone else's bottom half, and tape the schizo portrait together. Hang the finished photos on your youth bulletin board. These portraits will be quite an attraction.

TABLETOP PUBLICITY BOARDS

Short of bulletin board space? No bulletin boards period? Lean one or two six- or eight-foot folding tables up against the wall. You can tape announcements or whatever to the tabletops and avoid the damage that tape does to most walls. Or, creatively arrange two or three tables and add streamers and balloons to draw attention to the display. With a little muscle power, these publicity boards even become portable.

TITANIC ADVERTISING

Want to make a quality banner or huge poster but feel you can't draw? Use clip art, rub-on letters, and other graphic helps, and create your poster on blank white paper. Next, photocopy your creation to an overhead transparency.

Place the transparency on an overhead projector, and focus the image on to a large piece of butcher paper that is covering a large wall. Make sure the image fills the paper. Outline the images with black water-based paint and a medium-sized brush that allows you to keep detail. When you've finished, turn off the projector. Fill in the giant letters and figures with whatever colors of paint suit your design. This process also works for creating theatrical backdrops.

YARN BULLETIN BOARD

You will need long straight pins and rug yarn. Choose a yarn color that contrasts with your bulletin board's background. I usually use white on a darker color. On the two vertical sides of your bulletin board, equally space pins about 3" apart, the length of each side. Use the same number of pins on the horizontal sides, again spacing the pins 3" apart. If your board is rectangular, two of the sides won't have pins the whole length of the board. If your board is square, remove a few pins from the horizontal sides.

Take your ball of yarn and tie a loop in one end. Loop the end around the bottom left-hand corner pin, keeping the yarn out toward the head of the pin. Circle the whole board around the outer edges of the pins. You should end up with the shape of your board. Now, bring your yarn to the next pin over on the top row. Continue this by wrapping the yarn around the same pins on the other three sides, clockwise. Move to the next pin, and repeat this pattern with the rest of the pins. Pull out the yarn as close to the pinheads as you can. This will give more dimension. You now have a sharp design that seems to be alive. In the middle of the bulletin, attach a simple poster with the announcement on it.

Campus Access for Youth Ministry Promotion

appendix

A

J ay Sekulow, chief counsel with Atlanta-based Christian Advocates Serving Evangelism, and J. David Etheriedge, staff counsel with the American Center for Law and Justice in Washington, D.C., wrote an article titled, "Open Campus: How the Equal Access Law Affects You and Your Students" in the Summer 1993 issue of *Youthworker Journal*. In the article, the authors stated that they regularly receive letters and calls from youth leaders across the nation asking about the rights youth workers have in the public schools.

Wrote Sekulow and Etheriedge: "The answer to that question—'You have little or no right of access to public schools during the day'— discourages some youth workers. That discouragement can lead to an assumption that the public schools are gospel-free zones.

"That assumption is wrong. While outsiders enjoy few rights of access or expression during the school day, students themselves possess extremely broad free-speech rights."

Sekulow and Etheriedge go on to explain the Equal Access Act, citing specific cases as examples. In *Tinker v. Des Moines Independent Community School District 10*, the Supreme Court held that "students and teachers do not shed their First Amendment Rights when they enter the schoolhouse gate." As long as students rightfully belong on the school campus, the students have a right under the First Amendment to express their views. The same rules apply to students who wish to express their religious views on the public school campus.

The youth worker has no legal right to be on the public school campus. Students, however, have every legal right to express their faith, and promote youth group activities, as long as they don't violate other students' rights or disrupt the educational process.

If for some reason you need more information about the legal aspects of campus ministry, here are some suggestions.

• Read *Students' Legal Rights on a Public School Campus*, published by J. W. Brinkley, Roever Communications. For information call (817) 238-2005.

• Contact The American Center for Law and Justice, P. O. Box 64429, Virginia Beach, VA 23467. For more information call (404) 633-2444.

• Read *A Guide to the Equal Access Act*, published by the Center for Law and Religious Freedom, P. O. Box 1492, Merrifield, VA 22116. For more information call (703) 642-1070.

• Contact C.A.S.E. (Christian Advocates Serving Evangelism), P. O. Box 450349, Atlanta, GA 30345.

How to Use Video More Effectively

For those of you who know what a video camera is, but are afraid to use one, allow me to debunk a few commonly held myths about using video cameras in youth ministry. Again, Rick Bundschuh gave valuable advice in his book, *101 Things to Do with a Video Camera.*

MYTH 1: IT TAKES A TECHNICAL GENIUS TO USE A VIDEO CAMERA

The big reason for high-tech phobia is all the options, terms, and features video gear comes with—and it all changes monthly.

The good news is there's not a whole lot you need to understand about your video camera. Honest. All you need to know is how to point it and

---

shoot it—and, of course, how to keep it steady while you're pointing and shooting. But what about fade-ins and fade-outs, editing in titles, and other tricks? They're nice, but not essential.

Video equipment manufacturers are beginning to realize that they're selling their stuff to electronic plebeians who want to record a birthday party without first earning a college degree in electronics. That's why the new gear automatically does everything for you, except wipe your nose. Technology for the total idiot—like myself!

MYTH 2: VIDEO EQUIPMENT IS TOO EXPENSIVE

Expensive, of course, is a relative term. Compared to many other items, however, video gear is usually affordable for most church budgets. You can probably purchase a video camera with more features than you'll use in a year and still stay in budget.

Even if it's beyond your budget, video gear is almost certainly available to borrow. Almost every home now has a VCR, vast numbers of people own video cameras and some are charitable enough to loan them to their church's youth pastor. You can also rent video cameras from video stores.

MYTH 3: KIDS WILL ONLY WATCH PROFESSIONAL QUALITY VIDEOS

No matter how sophisticated they think they are, kids will watch anything if it's fast-paced, funny, or clever—and especially if they're in the video. They love to see themselves on TV. They could care less if it's Hollywood quality as long as they or someone they know are the stars.

MYTH 4: USING VIDEO MEANS HAULING AROUND LOTS OF EQUIPMENT

Some camcorders on the market are so small they can slip into a purse, yet they have everything you need to get an instant playback (except a TV).

Add a tripod (or, simpler yet, a monopod) to make sure you get smooth shots. There! You have all the gear you need.

MYTH 5: VIDEOS HAVE LITTLE SPIRITUAL VALUE

While fun itself is a good enough reason for me to break out the video camera, this medium can drive home spiritual truths, attract kids to the Gospel, record important decisions, and reinforce learning.

Resources

appendix C

BOOKS

YOUTH SPECIALTIES
1224 Greenfield Dr.
El Cajon, CA 92021
(619) 440-2333

Youth Specialties Clip Art Book
Youth Specialties Clip Art Book, Volume 2
ArtSource™ (book, IBM, MAC)
   The *ArtSource™* series is stuffed with current, easy-to-use art that gets promotional flyers noticed. It will help you create flyers, newsletters, calendars, and more.
Volume 1—Fantastic Activities
Volume 2—Borders, Symbols, Holidays, and Attention Getters
Volume 3—Sports
Volume 4—Phrases and Verses
Volume 5—Amazing Oddities and Appalling Images
Volume 6—Spiritual Topics

GROUP
P. O. Box 481
Loveland, CO 80539
(303) 669-3836

Classy Clip Art
Youth Ministry Clip Art
Outrageous Clip Art for Youth Ministry
Youth Ministry Care Cards
   • Affirmation (booklets)
   • Attendance Builders
   • Birthday Greetings
   • Esteem Builders
   • Visitors Follow-up
   • Volunteer Appreciation
Youth Ministry Clip Art Calendar
Cartoon Clip Art for Youth Leaders II

GOSPEL LIGHT PUBLISHING
2300 Knoll Drive
Ventura, CA 93003
(805) 644-9721

101 Outrageous Things to Do with a Video Camera (out of print)
The One Minute Poster
Youth Workers Clip Art Book
Super Clip Art for Youth Workers
Son of Clip Art Book

Magnetic Flyers
Kids Workers' Clip Art Book
I Was A Teenage Clip Art Book

PRODUCTS

Youth Specialties Youth Worker's Promo Kit
    The complete promotional and publicity kit for your ministry, it's designed to increase your creativity and save you time. It was created to be a complete "guessproof" promotional resource. It contains everything you need to create great looking and effective
- Calendars
- Newsletters
- Brochures
- Flyers
- Posters
- Tickets
- Letterheads
- Postcards

This little kit is a gold mine. It includes complete instructions, samples, and full-size layout patterns. It's an entire publicity department in a kit.
    Beginning Spring 1994, Youth Specialties will release annual Refill Packs for the *Promo Kit*.

SUPPLIERS, MANUFACTURERS, AND
MISCELLANEOUS BITS OF INFORMATION

You can order a button-making machine from Badge-a-Minit, 345 N. Lewis Ave, Box 800, Oglesby, IL 61348 or call 1-800-223-4103.

For printed messages on a pencil, calendar, ruler, comb, balloon, lollipop, wooden nickel, or just about anything, contact the Atlas Pen and Pencil Corporation, 3040 N. 29th Avenue, Hollywood, FL 33022.

If you have a small youth group, you can buy a minimum of ten engraved pens or pencils, bumper stickers with special messages, or a personalized three-line rubber stamp and ink pad from Miles Kimball, 41 East 8th Avenue, Oshkosh, WI 54901.

For $23, you can have a group member's face printed on a collection of paper dolls. Or for $28, you can have a special picture printed on the backs of a deck of cards. These are just two options in a mail-order catalog called *Exposures*. For a free catalog, call 1-800-222-4947 outside New Jersey. Call 1-201-370-8110 if you live in New Jersey.

Have your favorite youth group shot mounted on the face of a red, blue, black, or white Timex watch for around $30. For information, call 1-800-FOR-TIMEX.

For printing your summer calendar on water bottles (or sport bottles) call Countryside Products, Box 13256, Columbus, OH 43213 at 1-614-861-6116.

Blank pre-cut puzzling notes are available in sets of 15 with envelopes in a gift box for $14.95 by dialing 1-800-362-5500. Ask for item #04-D-0259.

For a company that will print your logo on painters' caps, call American Mills in Minneapolis for prices and a catalogue at 1-800-876-4287.

Here's a list of T-Shirt designers and companies:

Designer Unlimited
P. O. Box 9813
Panama City Beach, FL 32417
904-235-3262
1-800-919-6884

Carousel Productions
11000 Wilcrest, Suite 100
Houston, TX 77099
713-568-9300

Church Art Works
875 High Street NE
Salem, OR 97301
503-370-9377

Keith Poletiek
Yahwear
15230 Ashwood Ln.
Chino Hills, CA 91709
409-597-4862

Living Epistles
P.O. Box 77777
Klamath Falls, OR 97601
1-800-874-4790

INDEX